BEYOND OUR TRIBAL GODS

The Maturing of Faith

Ronald Marstin

ORBIS BOOKS

Maryknoll, New York 10545

Second Printing, February 1982

The Catholic Foreign Mission Society of America (Maryknoll) recruits and trains people for overseas missionary service. Through Orbis Books Maryknoll aims to foster the international dialogue that is essential to mission. The books published, however, reflect the opinions of their authors and are not meant to represent the official position of the society.

Library of Congress Cataloging in Publication Data

Marstin, Ronald.
  Beyond our tribal gods.

  Bibliography: p.
  1. Faith. 2. Faith—Psychology. 3. Christian
life—Catholic authors. 4. Sociology, Christian
(Catholic) I. Title.
BT771.2M28   261.8'5   79-4354
ISBN 0-88344-030-X

BEYOND OUR TRIBAL GODS

CONTENTS

Foreword

Few can remain unaware today of the raised voices of the world's poor. Nor is there any mistaking their demand—to share as equals in a new world community.

The decisions we take in response to that demand will be decisions taken in faith. That is to say, they will be made according to some definition of what it means to be holy, and, for Christians, some definition of what it means to be faithful to the Gospel.

To know what holiness means and what is meant by fidelity to the Gospel it seems helpful to have some understanding of the path that faith takes as it grows and matures. I hope that this book will contribute to that understanding.

It is addressed and dedicated to all those—parents, pastors, teachers, and preachers of the Word—who would foster a faith adequate to our times, a faith to celebrate the new world community.

Thanks are due especially to two people who once taught me at Harvard Divinity School. Professor James W. Fowler introduced me to his pioneering research into the development of faith. Sister Marie Augusta Neal pressed upon me the sociological questions with which an analysis of faith development must deal. More than that, both teachers gave me the example of their own fidelity.

New York City

CHAPTER 1

The Challenge to Faith

Insiders and Outsiders

Around here, people are worried. This is what the social scientists would call an urban ethnic neighborhood. We call it home. Or at least we used to, for it looks and feels less like home every year. Everything is changing—the faces, the accents, the foodstuffs in the supermarket, the physical appearance of the place, the texture of social life—and nobody thinks it is changing for the better. Whispered street-corner conversations angrily catalogue the deterioration, the increase in crime, the rising tide of our fears. As the edges of the ghetto press outward, encroaching day by day on what used to be "our" turf, we feel increasingly beleaguered. And another crude graffito appears overnight on a nearby wall: *Niggers Beware!*

Ours is one of those parishes that still ring out the *Angelus* three times a day—an old, familiar pattern, morning, noon, and again at night. It always sounds a bit incongruous. Nobody that I know actually remembers the prayer anymore. In fact, thanks to an electrical timing device in the church steeple, no one need even remember to ring the bell. But, not altogether unlike the medieval churchbell rallying the

1

villagers in time of calamity, it serves as a token of
solidarity in troubled times, a sign of holding-on in
time of threat, to the community, its way of life, its
values and traditions. Certainly, it is a reminder that
the parish church never exists in a vacuum. When the
bells are rung, the faithful called to worship, the faith
proclaimed, it is always in a concrete social context.
Around here that context is fear of the spreading
blight.

There is nothing exclusively urban, ethnic, working-class, or Catholic about racism. Indeed, sociologist Andrew M. Greeley has recently amassed impressive evidence to suggest that ethnic Catholics are
less racist than comparable groups among the general population.[1] Certainly, zoning restrictions in
suburban communities that prevent the construction of racially integrated housing for people with
low and moderate incomes reflect a racism as per-
vasive as any in the cities. Moreover, urban ethnic
communities are understandably angered by pro-
nouncements and policies shaped for them by suburban liberals when it is the urban neighborhood that is
most immediately threatened with deterioration and
there that jobs are at stake. While the urban neighborhood is for me closest to home, and its fears of our
impoverished black and Hispanic neighbors the
easiest to document from personal experience, this is
not to suggest that we are atypical in this regard, but
rather that we are typical of all those who find that
what they have (and what they have often struggled
hard to acquire) is threatened by those who have less.

The differences between haves and have-nots, in
fact, turn out frequently to be more decisive than
differences of color. The neighborhood organizing of
block clubs, for example, which has been growing in

many cities, often with the support of the parishes, has produced some impressive coalitions of black and white homeowners around such issues as disinvestment and redlining on the part of banks. It is in no way to deny the positive contributions of these coalitions to the solution of real problems of urban working-class people to note that, at the same time, they easily generate a new solidarity against the poor, unemployed, sometimes militant and sometimes unruly group that Whitney Young once called "the growing black underclass."

Whether it takes the form of clear social-class lines, or of racial or sex lines, the fundamental problem is one of boundaries—and often barricades—between those struggling to have what they lack and need and those trying to hang on to what they have. It is not just an urban problem, any more than the division between haves and have-nots is just an urban phenomenon. It is a world problem. We live in a world marked by boundaries: economic boundaries, dividing the comfortable from the poor; political boundaries, dividing the powerful from the powerless; social boundaries, dividing those reckoned to matter from those reckoned not to matter.

It is true that all these categories—of haves and have-nots, powerful and powerless, insiders and outsiders—are somewhat relative. People who are "in" in some respects may be "out" in other respects, and vice versa. (In the study already noted, for example, Greeley argues that the ethnic Catholic is now "in" in terms of education and family income, though still "out" at the upper levels of business, professional, and academic life.) But, especially where it is a question of such basic human needs as adequate food, shelter, and health care, the categories are by no

means meaningless. Quite simply, some people have
access to these things and some do not. There is a line
to be drawn. According to Dom Helder Camara,
Archbishop of Olinda-Recife in northeast Brazil and
one of the world's most credible spokesmen for the
poor, that line separates the more or less affluent
one-third of the world's population—perhaps a billion
and a half—from the needy two-thirds—more than
two and a half billion. On this division, if we are white,
working, and living in a developed nation, we are insiders. Most of the world's people, including the
poorest in our own country, are outsiders. What side
of the line people happen to fall on will likely determine for them their most basic preoccupation in
life—on the one side, people struggle to get what they
need; on the other, to hang on to what they have.
Moreover, to the extent that what *we* have is what
they need, our hanging on to what we have will mean
keeping them out.

A New World Order?

This issue had never before been raised as pointedly
as it was in 1974 when, as the result of a growing
solidarity among 112 of the world's poor nations, the
United Nations issued a call for a "new international
economic order." The storm had been brewing for a
long time. Back in the mid-fifties, when the world was
divided into two hostile camps, communist and "free
world," a few dozen southern nations met in Ban-
dung, Indonesia, and declared themselves "non-
aligned." They were for the most part nations that
had recently won their political independence from
the powerful nations of the north but found themselves still economically dependent on those nations.

They had not yet experienced an industrial revolution; they were financially unsophisticated; they were poor.

In the last twenty years, however, they have grown —in numbers, in their consciousness of the ties that bind them together, and in strength. They have become known as the "Third World"—over against the "First World" of western capitalism and the "Second World" of the Soviet-bloc nations—and they have made it increasingly clear that the way the world's business is presently conducted is intolerable to them. They will no longer accept "solutions" to their problems foisted on them by the rich nations in "development" and "aid" programs that leave them worse off than before. They want a change in the rules that presently give control over most of the earth's resources to a minority of the world's people. They want to share as equal partners in the decisions about how those resources will be used and their benefits distributed. They want a new, a fair, world order.

So far, the powerful nations have resisted most of the concrete proposals of the developing nations for a fairer deal, such as stabilizing the prices of their commodity exports rather than leaving them to the caprices of the marketplace (where fluctuations can destroy the fragile economy of a poor nation and make any rational economic planning impossible for them), renegotiating debts or canceling them outright where a country has been driven into a hopeless situation, permitting easier access to world markets, nationalizing foreign-owned property (with compensation paid according to local law), or forming producers' associations (as the oil-exporting countries have done). For the time being, we have a choice. We can keep re-

sisting—at least as long as we have the power—
or we can stop resisting. We can fight any change
in the status quo or we can begin to dismantle the
global economic system that has dominated the
world for a century and that is clearly stacked
against most of the world's people. We can struggle
to maintain our competitive advantage or we can
work cooperatively to build a new order geared to
the welfare of the four billion people with whom we
share the earth.

Critical Issue for Faith

That is how the major issue of our times is shaping
up. It becomes sharper the more we discover the
limits of the world's natural resources. It is likely to
be around for a long time, the main item on the
agenda for ourselves and our children. As such, it is
the main issue with which we must deal as people of
faith. For faith has no world of its own. As people
trying to keep the faith and teach it to a new generation, we are always practicing it in the actual world, a
world that inevitably sets the agenda for faith. Today
this is, most characteristically, a world in which the
poor challenge the rich for the right to live as respected equals. In Asia, Africa, and Latin America, on
the islands of the South Pacific and in the urban ghet-
toes of the industrialized world, people are beginning
to rise up to demand and take what they claim is
theirs—and people are digging in to protect what they
have. There are all the makings here of a terrible
struggle. In fact there are more than the makings, for
the violence on our borders, in our streets, and in our
hearts is the battle already joined. There is no escap-
ing it; we are drawn into it whether we like it or not.
We choose sides; or we simply inherit sides. Wherever

people today strive to be faithful to their religious traditions, it is this divided, conflicted world that provides the arena for their striving. It is this world in which faith will make a difference, one way or the other, shaping for the poor their challenge, shaping for the affluent their response.

What is the faithful response to a world in which some are treated unfairly? What is faith's answer to injustice? Ever since Job reflected on the meaning of undeserved evil, this has been a major question for faith. Any faith tradition—as an interpretation of the *whole* human experience, an attempt to set things in their ultimate context—must give some accounting for the universal, persistent experience of injustice. The way we finally interpret the world—including whatever sense we make of the world's injustice—will determine what we find morally tolerable, what we feel moved to change, what we find absolutely sacred, what we consider dispensable, what we are able to hope for, what kind of response will alone justify our lives. Different traditions sometimes espouse quite different interpretations and so result in quite different priorities. A major difference lies in the fundamental attitude faith takes toward this world. How seriously is it to be taken? In answering that question, different faith traditions can foster contrasting attitudes to the world. A faith can foster an attitude of engagement or one of withdrawal. It can foster flight or involvement. It can expose or insulate. It can impel a person to change the world or it can help one simply to cope with it.

This World Matters

For some of the classic religions of the East the visible world is ephemeral, illusory, of no concern.

These traditions focus the attention and care of the faithful on the unchanging order of the universe that is said to lie behind the violence and lust of the temporal world, encouraging them to withdraw from the unseemly hubbub of the one to find peace in contemplating the other. That is not the Christian way. What is peculiar about Christianity is that obedience to God is understood to involve the collective task of remaking this world.[2] In our tradition this world matters. Nor is it any accident that the tradition has taken on such a this-worldly, incarnational stance: it runs to the very heart of our faith. Christianity's concern for the divided, violent world is linked at its roots to the monotheism that it has inherited from Judaism—the belief in one God transcending all the gods of tribe and nation, in whose sight all the peoples of the world are people who matter.

A special feel for history underpins the Jewish-Christian tradition. According to the classic Greek view, the world is essentially changeless. History is a series of cycles, endlessly repeating itself. Nothing really new can be expected. Time is barren, its passage meaningless. Only space is meaningful: territory, soil, blood, race. A certain kind of religion—usually termed "priestly" religion—celebrates and strengthens that view of the world. Priestly religion is the religion of people bound to the hallowed land, a religion to sanction the borders. A people trusts its god to protect its turf. By contrast, the Jewish worldview was dynamic, understanding history as a continuous unfolding that God disrupts with "mighty works," and time as pregnant with possibilities. Even more important than blood-ties was the historical covenant with God. This view of the world is celebrated by a different kind of religion, usually termed "prophetic." Prophetic religion is that of people detached from the soil, people on the move, people with a historical task to do, a task to transcend borders.[3]

One and Only God

This distinction has much to do with the kind of attitude sponsored by faith toward a divided world. That some peoples arc pitted against others, insiders barring their gates against outsiders, does not necessarily pose any problem for a purely priestly religion. In the Old Testament, the priests instructed the people in the law and offered the sacrifice. That is, it was their task to socialize members into the group's established way of life and to affirm the group as holy in God's eyes. It was only the *prophet* who questioned this assumption that God's blessing was still upon the gathered people.[4]

In essence, the prophetic message is that simply to maintain the group's established way of life is not enough to guarantee God's blessing. It is not enough just to hang on to the traditional ways. Where God is seen to be a God for *all* the world's people, and not simply "our" God, then it is the task of the prophet to expose the faithlessness of maintaining a way of life that protects some but excludes others. This is the difference between the false and the true prophet: while the false prophet claims that the covenant binds God unconditionally and perpetually to this people, the true prophet recognizes that the covenant puts the people under judgment.[5] For the people of the one-and-only God are never simply this people or that people: the people of God are all the peoples of the world.

Here was something quite distinctive among the

religions of the ancient world. For, while it emerged historically as the faith of a particular people, it carried seeds of hope for all peoples. While it frequently resembled other tribal and national faiths, which frankly called upon their gods to protect their own and strengthen them for the slaughter of their enemies, it also broke with this pattern. For Yahweh was not finally one tribal god among many, but the One God before whom there stood no other. Here was a universal faith, celebrating the God whose dominion encompassed all. The narrower peoplehood of Israel would now be situated within this wider peoplehood, its claim to God's loving concern based not on an exclusive membership in the company of the elect but on membership in the human race.

Social Justice

For this reason, God could now be recognized as the guarantor of *human* rights, those rights to protection and respect accruing equally to all people and solely on the basis of their humanity. For the same reason, the worship of God would be inextricably tied to the quality of our care for one another, for the stranger as for our own. Social justice would emerge as an essential strand of the faith tradition, its prophets periodically calling the people to account for the rules—the political, social, and economic institutions—that framed their common life. Where people are called to the worship of a God whose love is understood to embrace all the world's people, then the essential idolatry lies in accepting as God's will a social arrangement in which the lives of some are reckoned cheap.

It is easy to overlook the special character of the

concern for human rights that finds its basis in the Jewish-Christian tradition. Many have coopted the language of human rights and the related language of social justice. At least during his early months in office, President Carter's foreign policy statements returned to the "human rights" issue more consistently than to any other theme. And there is surely no earthly regime without some vaunted allegiance to the principles of "social justice." The fact, of course, is that the labels can mean very different things, most of them quite compatible with maintaining a blatantly oppressive social order.

Among the classical Greeks, for example, justice was linked with the notion of merit—all should get what they deserve, though some are more deserving than others—a notion that survives in our current distinction between the deserving and the undeserving poor.[6] In more recent formulations, justice has come variously to stand for the rule of *quid pro quo* (what you get should be proportionate to what you contribute),[7] or respect for property rights,[8] or for the orderly society (in which the unruly passions of the common people are held in check),[9] or even reduced—in a newly-popular interpretation—to the biological strategy by which "successful" genes keep reproducing themselves.[10] Given this kind of definition, justice may guarantee much less than the worth of all persons and their right to equal treatment: it may simply lend legitimacy to established inequalities.

Even when justice is linked seriously with some understanding of the inalienable dignity of all human beings, it has sometimes come to focus on an exclusive category of rights, as in the preference of western constitutional democracies for stressing political and civil rights (such as freedom of speech and assembly) over social and economic rights (such as a fair share in the earth's resources of food and energy). In the competitive society, even the guarantee of an "equality of opportunity" by no means guarantees to people any equality in their use of the common wealth. Biblical justice, on the other hand, names the human community in which none is inferior to another.

Reclaiming Our Meanings

The lesson of history in this regard is that even our most promising symbols of human fellowship are vulnerable to constant redefinition in a way that dilutes the universalist aspirations they originally embodied and harnesses their power in the interests of those who presently enjoy the advantage. The symbols that promise hope to the excluded are coopted to the benefit of those already included. Even the religious tradition that claims special responsibility for preserving and celebrating these symbols has allowed them to be so corrupted and distorted. In the Israel into which Jesus was born, the kingdom of God—once a radical vision of the just and peaceful society—had become largely synonymous with the social institutions of the nation. Jesus would challenge this identification by his own rejection of the nation's religious and political authorities and his fresh insistence that the dignity of all is protected only when the least powerful are embraced. Soon enough, however, Christian empires would be reinterpreting Jesus' message for their own political purposes.

Apparently it takes the clamor of the excluded to jolt the included into any recognition of the gap between the values they profess and the political systems they tolerate. Today the raised voices of the Third World are awakening the church to the incongruity of its proclaiming the "good news to the poor" while it collaborates with the systems that oppress them. The first fruits of this new awakening at the level of the official church have been a series of documents issued in recent years that forthrightly (if not always consistently) define as essential to the Christian life a concerted effort to transform the global economic, political, and social structures that oppress people.[11] Individual charity is recognized as no substitute for the struggle to build the just society. Nor can the church's time-honored commitment to serving the victims of oppression excuse our failure to remedy the *causes* of their oppression.

International Church, Neighborhood Church

Reference to the church's redefinition of its global mission raises the obvious question of who is meant when we speak of "the church," and specifically of the relationship between the official, international institution and the local communities of the faithful. For if the renewed emphasis in the official teachings on the social and political implications of the Gospel signifies some growing sensitivity to the needs of the local churches in Africa, Asia, and Latin America, there is some evidence of a sizable gap in consciousness between the international bodies and local churches nearer home. Even on the national level, the general lack of communication between the churches' national headquarters and their local parishes sometimes suggests that the two groups have different agenda, different priorities, perhaps different definitions of the church's mission. It is possible to see this as essentially a communications problem, one of inept leadership, bureaucratic insensitivity, and inadequate popular representation in the church. A plausible case can be made for this interpretation and *Humanae Vitae*, the 1968 "pill" encyclical, is sometimes cited as a striking symbol of the problem.[12]

Some attention should be given to the possibility, however, that the problem here is not simply one of communications but one of substance, that is, to the possibility that the new summons from the church leadership has indeed been heard and, more or less consciously, rejected by parishioners locked into earlier definitions of the church's mission or simply caught up in other tasks. The question raised here is not primarily a question about anybody's sincerity. It is not a question about good will, energy, or zeal. It is a question about what the faithful in the local diocese and parish are actually doing, and why they are doing it. And it is a question of what all this has to do with the summons to remake the world in justice.

Why We Go to Church

In fact, the reasons why Christians gather in their neighborhood churches have been the subject of considerable research, originally sparked by a need to explain the acquiescence of Christians in the Nazi persecution of the Jews. Of special concern has been the part played by the local church in the tendency of people to identify "their own" and to exclude the stranger. One early study of prejudice suggested that Christians find in the parish an "island of safety" on which to gather in solidarity against outsiders,[13] a troubling assessment, but one given weight by several subsequent studies.[14] Especially since the bur-

geoning of the civil rights movement in the U.S. in the
fifties, the issue of racial prejudice has been recognized as a critical challenge to the churches and the
response of churchgoers to that challenge as a central
indicator of what is happening when they gather for
worship in the neighborhood parish.

For a time Christian ministry did in some places
take up the challenge of bringing the Gospel to bear
on issues of racial justice, although as early as 1957
some sociologists were predicting that, in the long
run, fear of losing money and church members would
persuade local clergy to shift the focus of their ministry from issues of justice back to issues of interest to
the existing parish community.[15]

This prediction was made at the high point of
church membership in the U.S., but it was to prove
only too accurate, and the long run turned out to be
not too long a run at all. By 1970, after a decade of
liberal activism, church membership was at the low
point of a rapid decline. The birth control encyclical of
1968 does not explain this disaffection. For one thing,
it affected many churches for which birth control was
not an issue; and, for another, the falling-away began
ten years before the encyclical. The decline was diag-
nosed in 1972 as due among other things to the liberal
churches' move in the direction of social involvement.[16] Recovery of membership and financial support, the same researcher predicted, would follow
a return of the churches to other-wordly concerns,
a turning away from political involvement, and a
refocusing of ministry on individual commitment
within the context of the local community. It is
perhaps too early to tell, but the recent growth of the
conservative churches and of the charismatic movement—with its focus, by and large, on inner trans-

formation, warm interpersonal bonding, and the repudiation of action for social change in favor of a charity defined as one-on-one service—suggests that this prediction, too, may be accurate.[17]

For twenty years the most pressing issue for the churches has been how to respond to the pleas, the demands, of the world's excluded peoples that they be enabled to share as equals in the life of the nations and the international community. The local church has prayed for the poor and given money for their relief. It has debated whether critical reflection on the rules of society is not after all the church's business. Sometimes it has anguished over the rules that exclude the poor and the racial minorities. But when it comes down to *changing* the rules, the local church is often found busy with other matters.

How diverse are the activities, concerns and lifestyles embraced by the churches! Clearly, even within a single religious tradition, believers may be about many different things. Contemporary Catholicism includes sober Sunday Massgoers and armed revolutionaries; Knights of Columbus dressed up for their faith, Fr. Rutilio Grande gunned down for his; suburban couples, fresh from Marriage Encounter, hand-in-hand for Communion; Jesuits in El Salvador threatened with death for their work among the nation's peasants; bishops of the people—like Mexico's Ruiz and Brazil's Camara—and Curial monsignori in dark glasses, skilled in the *Realpolitik* of eastern Europe; shuffling peasants in a thousand gaudy shrines to Our Lady; charismatic communities high on enthusiasm in Ann Arbor and Providence; in Washington, D.C., the Community for Creative Non-Violence, bent on common struggle with the poor; in decaying urban churches, elderly women telling their beads before statues of St. Anthony; pontifical Mass for a military junta in Chile or a colonial power in New Caledonia; in the California fields, a burial Mass for a slain Chicano farmworker; bishops denying women's rights in Rome, and defending workers in Peru; sisters teaching third grade catechism, running for Congress, ministering to the sick, or organizing the J. P. Stevens boycott; right-to-lifers and block club organizers; Dorothy Day and Mother Teresa; Geno Baroni and the monks of Solesmes; Pope John Paul II and Arlo Guthrie. What is to be made of such diversity?

Defining the Church's Mission

Surely there is a legitimate place for pluralism within the church, room for diverse initiatives, styles of life and ministry. But, just as surely, we are working from different and sometimes incompatible definitions of the church's mission, inspired by different and sometimes incompatible models of holiness. Can all definitions be equally valid, all responses equally faithful to the Gospel? Here we need to return to our roots in the tradition. In a sense, it is a question of orthodoxy. It is a question with which we are frequently reluctant to deal, mindful of the often oppressive certitudes of the past, of Inquisitions, intolerance, and the absolutes that kill. We have learned to settle for an easier relativism, a celebration of the freedom "to do one's own thing."

But relativism can be deadly, too. When systems are so structured that millions of people are condemned to die or to beg for their existence, the easy relativism that disperses the energies of Christians in a dozen different directions is an instrument of their death and degradation. Already, hard-headed strategies are being devised to deal with the urgent problems of how to conserve and distribute the earth's scarce resources, including the "triage" policy, which would discard a third of the world's population as beyond help, or the "lifeboat ethics," which would sacrifice justice to the demands of "reality."[18] Should the lifeboat become our guiding image for dealing with the problem of hunger and triage our preferred strategy, a vision of faith will be needed to legitimate the hard choices to be made. Inevitably, religion will be called upon to provide an ultimate justification for abandoning those whom we choose to abandon. A relativistic religion will prove sufficiently flexible to provide the needed rationale.

It is precisely because the Jewish-Christian tradition will suffer none to be abandoned—because all are God's people—that it is no relativistic tradition. The tradition has content and its content is sharp-edged. In a fresh statement of the ancient biblical command "to break unjust fetters, to undo the thongs of the yoke, to let the oppressed go free" (Isa. 50:3), the third Synod of Bishops speaks of action to transform oppressive social structures as "a constitutive dimension" of Gospel preaching and church mission.[19] For the Christian, such action is not simply one alternative in a whole range of possible lifestyles: it is an essential characteristic of Gospel faith. That faith, no doubt, embraces other concerns as well, but these remain incomplete as long as they remain unrelated to the struggle for justice. As long as our service to the poor remains unrelated to the causes of their poverty, our inner transformations unrelated to the transformation of the world, our prayer unrelated to the

struggle for the just society, they represent inadequate responses to the contemporary challenge of
faith: for in this manner are well-intentioned initiatives coopted to the maintenance of the oppressive
society. The refusal to be so coopted is a critical test of
fidelity.

The Yardstick Is Justice

Whatever we are doing in the local diocese, parish,
school, or religious order will need to be measured
against this yardstick. In the face of social injustice
we are summoned to proclaim the injustice, to help
one another become disentangled from the oppressive
system, and to build the new society in the interests of
all. Failing that, the church remains itself simply a
part of the unjust society, the local parish one more
institution feeding the oppressive system. Once injustice is seen to exist, should the churches ignore it,
define it as too large a problem to tackle, feel overwhelmed by it, or simply give priority to other tasks,
then whatever they are busy with will no longer be
the works of faith.

We inevitably stand somewhere on this issue. We
either stand for actively resisting the unjust system
or we stand for business more or less as usual. We can
easily tell where we stand by listening to what is
typically preached in our churches and taught in our
schools and catechetical programs about the central
challenges of the Christian life. Does that teaching
and preaching help people to keep investing their
emotional energy in a system that wearies them and
exploits the poor, or does it prepare them to resist it?
Does it lead to transforming action on the world or

does it save us from having to take such action by
focusing our attention on some quite different set of
concerns?

Our answers to these questions will reveal the
working definitions implicit in every aspect of local
church life: in policy statements, the setting of goals
and priorities, the way decisions are made, the lines of
accountability, the style of our teaching, preaching,
and pastoral counseling, the use of our resources, the
content of the parish bulletin, the focus of the
monthly baptism instruction, the tasks that are
funded and those that remain undone. Implicit in all
these areas are definitions of the church and its mission, the nature of the kingdom of God, the prin-
cipalities and powers against which the believer's
struggle is waged, the Christian life. Every facet of
parish life reflects some definition of the people of
God, those we recognize as "our" people, to whose
interests our ministry is geared and whose life-
experience finds expression in our gathering for worship and reflection.

We will not have to look far to see whose life-
experience is taken seriously in our local church. We
will not have to listen long to see whose questions get
addressed. We need only attend to our liturgies, to the
values that are affirmed there, the lives that are
celebrated, the causes that are espoused or avoided,
the action that results or fails to result. Are the lives
and causes of the world's oppressed and excluded
peoples coming to expression there? Recall the last
issue to galvanize the parish into action: whose interests were at stake? Look to see who the people are
who gather in our churches because the church is
responsive to their needs, and to see those who do not

gather because to them the church is irrelevant or a scandal.

Every aspect of parish life points to our implicit definition of what it is that we are fundamentally about as members of the church, our understanding of what it means to be faithful, our model of holiness. How we assess the goals and achievements of the local diocese or parish will depend on that definition. Just as the faith tradition is not infinitely malleable, neither is every image of the faithful person equally true to the tradition. The tradition carries its own criterion of fidelity and the criterion is justice.

CHAPTER 2

How Faith Develops

Faith a Process of Development

Leaving aside the specifically Christian ideal, can we learn anything about the meaning of mature faithfulness by looking at the development of faith in general? The very idea that faith might be said to *develop* is already worth a second look. For one thing, it pulls us beyond the notion that faith is something that a person simply has or does not have, and even beyond the notion that faith is a quantity of which a person can have more or less. For it includes here several fresh claims: first, that people can have faith in a number of quite different ways; second, that people *grow* in faith, growing out of one way of being faithful and into a new way, and, therefore, that some ways of being faithful can be said to be more developed or mature than others. The idea of development holds out the promise of new insight into the varieties of faith.

An idea that has captured the imagination of a number of social scientists in recent years is that of common *life-stages*. The idea is that, as we each trace our individual journeys from birth to the grave, we pass through a regular sequence of stages. We may sometimes get hung up at a particular stage, find the transition to a new stage exhilarating or bewildering, feel isolated or encouraged in the process, feel ourselves drawing nearer to or further from our spouses and friends; but—whatever the mix of fear and hope we bring to it—the passage from stage to stage is seen as the basic model of human growth and development. The recent popularity of books like Gail Sheehy's *Passages* suggests that many people have found in this "stage theory" a useful tool for interpreting their life-histories. Some theologians have begun to wonder if it might not also prove useful in explaining the development of faith. If we grow to maturity as persons through a series of distinct stages, and if faith is an integral part of our personal lives, may not faith be expected to mature by the same process?

A couple of assumptions underlie this theory. The first is that the social sciences could have something to teach us about faith—in other words, that, as a quality of human beings, faith might be expected to develop according to the usual rules of human development. This may prove less troublesome to Catholics than to Protestants. Catholics are, after all, long familiar with the Thomistic axiom that grace builds on nature, whereas many Protestants have traditionally emphasized the profound distinction between the "works of God" and the "works of man." Without ignoring the distinction, the new faith research does rather stress the connection. What is assumed here is that while faith is God's gift, freely given, it is nevertheless given in a way that respects our humanity. We are graced in a way that does not override but takes up our human ways of responding. While faith signifies an altogether special area of human existence and cannot be *reduced* to personal qualities—mental skills, role-taking ability, emotional maturity, or the like—neither is growth in faith *unrelated* to growth in these areas. While faith is frequently nourished by a religious tradition with its own claim to truth, its own integrity and authority, the way that the traditional beliefs are incorporated and personalized by the individual believer depends on the believer's maturity as a person. Though the gift is divine, the recipient is human. Though the graciousness of God is unchanging, the believer is caught up in a lifelong process of development. How far the believer has traveled on that developmental journey will be reflected in the quality of his or her faith. That is one assumption.

A second assumption behind this search for the general laws of faith's development is that it can make sense to talk about faith *in general*, that is, regardless of the particular faith traditions in which people are customarily brought up. Catholics may balk at this notion, for many of us came to understand long ago that faith *is* the tradition. Back in the forties, in deploring the shoddy thinking of the time—an intellectual sloppiness said to be infecting even the Catholic church—Monsignor (as he was then) Fulton Sheen used an expression as characteristic of the Catholicism of the time as it was of the man himself. "The trouble," he growled, "is that there are no enemies worthy of the church's steel." No enemies worthy of our steel. Our gladiators slipshod for want of competition. It was a stirring image, of a faith tried in battle, of steel on steel, of truths cut sharp in a glorious history of intellectual debate. But where was the competition today that would sharpen our wits as the Docetists once did, or the Monophysites, or the Reformers? We were reduced to namby-pamby sparring with agnostics, relativists, nominalists, and pragmatists, opponents with no real stomach for the clash of rational disputation!

These were heady times for Catholics. It was an era of confidence, not to say arrogance, in our finely-honed certitudes, and of security in the knowledge that there was an irrefutable Catholic answer to every question. On the other side of the coin, of course, was the fear of losing—of losing an argument, and so losing the faith. For this was what faith was about, a body of truths revealed in the sacred texts and sharpened in theological debate down through the ages; an edifice of interlocking doctrines about the existence of God, the divinity of Christ, the marks of the true church, papal infallibility, grace and sacrament, sin and virtue, punishment and reward. By faith—or "the faith" as we usually put it—we meant our beliefs, those statements about God to which we gave our assent, our creed.

Actually, while the chapter on faith in our traditional catechisms customarily began by comparing faith to our *experience of trust or reliance* upon others, it moved quickly to the reliability of the spokespersons recorded in the sacred scripture and tradition and from there to the *body of propositions* they had bequeathed us. Such expressions as "to have the faith," "to pass on the faith," and "to lose one's faith" then referred to having, passing on, and losing that body of propositions. Any of us who have left for college backed by parental admonitions to be careful about what we read—for fear of endangering our faith—will be familiar with that use of the term.

Only fairly recently in western theology has it become apparent that faith cannot be simply identified with beliefs. One of the main reasons this became clear was the discovery by nineteenth-century anthropologists that many nonwestern civilizations, and preliterate societies as well, have long enjoyed a very rich religious life without ever having put together a canon of revealed truths or any kind of theological edifice. Doctrinal systems simply do not figure much in the religious life of these peoples. This discovery has helped us to see that the identification of faith with creed is something peculiar to our own cultural tradition.[1] Consequently, we have been pressed to see faith as a reality more profound than a body of information, or a "bag of truths," that can be won or lost. In fact, many theologians have come to see faith as a more or less universal feature of human life, a quality intimately bound up with our existence as selves. Nor does the fact that we need not be conscious of it make this quality any the less important in shaping our lives and decisions.

Our Faith and Our Beliefs

As a rule, we are not forced often to reflect on the very basic meanings that ground our lives. We are usually caught up in a plethora of more immediate concerns that keep us busy enough. There is work to be done, there are children to be cared for, appointments to be kept, immediate problems to be solved, days ahead to be planned. There is even theology to be done, propositions about God to be hammered out in scholarly discussion. In other words, there is usually reason enough in the tasks we have to do to keep us acting purposefully from one day to another—until the bottom drops out of our world. It might be the tragedy that shakes us to the foundations, a random succession of mishaps pushing us to the limits of our ability to cope, bewildering evils at home or abroad, or simply a deep and undefined boredom. Old ideas now seem hollow; old certitudes have broken down; old passions are cold. We find ourselves overwhelmed, exposed, no longer able to make sense of things.

It is then that we are pressed to that outer perimeter of meaning that encloses all our meanings. We are forced back to the very root convictions about the reason for our existence, about the kind of universe we inhabit and the meaning of our place within it. It is in terms of these convictions that things must finally make sense if our lives are to make any sense at all. Not to be able to put it all together on this ultimate level is to find ourselves face-to-face with that terrible emptiness known as despair. On the other hand, to have touched the depths and yet to have risen with a meaning to live by is to have found faith. We may even have found a creed. Not all will find a system of belief, however. And still fewer will find our system. But all must find faith.

Behind all the day-to-day tasks, expectations, and responsibilities that make up the usual framework of our lives there is—as we discover when events force us to fall back on it—a more basic framework of accountability. Beneath the surface meanings there is a foundation of meaning, a certain conviction about, a certain feel for, the whole that encompasses us. This is the depth dimension of our lives, the realm of faith. Theologian Paul Tillich calls it "the ultimate concern in all our preliminary concerns, . . . the inexhaustible meaning in everything that has meaning."[2]

When we try to express this "inexhaustible meaning" that grounds our lives, we find ourselves struggling to contain it in words, in statements, or—when we find our efforts halting and inarticulate—in symbols, images, and metaphors that point to what we are trying to express. Of course, we rarely struggle as individuals. We have a culture, a language, to work with. Usually, we have the beliefs and symbols of some religious tradition to draw upon, the testimony of generations of witnesses on whom we have learned to rely, a testimony frequently recorded in written texts long held sacred and worthy of trust. Once this happens, our faith takes on a particular content, our ultimate concern is given a name. The way Tillich puts it is that "faith is the state of being grasped by an ultimate concern, and God is the name for the content of that concern."[3]

Not to have the experience of an unconditional truth beneath our derived and conditional truths would be to feel our feet on no firm ground. It would be to find all our meanings coming unstuck, to find our lives with no direction at all, to feel our selves disintegrate. For faith in this sense is part of what it means to be a self. Faith is the self as the self owns up to its most basic loyalty. It names our most fundamental orientation and colors the way we see everything that we see: the universe, the point of our existence, the society of which we are part, the meaning that other persons have for us. Understood in this sense, it is not something "tacked on" to our lives, like a bag of truths picked up along the way, but an essential element of our experience of what it is to be a human being.

The difference between this sense we have of an ultimate accountability and the particular symbols in which we express it is the difference between our faith and our beliefs. Because of this difference we may share with others the experience of faith even when we do not have any beliefs in common with them. Beliefs are particular; faith is universal. If we disentangle faith as a universal quality of human

existence from the various beliefs and rituals through
which it is apt to be expressed, we are able to think
about faith in a new way. We are able to speak of faith
as a quality of human beings rather than as the property of a particular church. We are able to seek out its
universal features rather than simply cataloguing its
many particular expressions. Setting aside the *content* of specific beliefs and systems of belief, we are
able to focus more broadly on people's *ways of believing*. From the *what* of faith, our attention moves to the
how of faith.

Different Ways of Being Faithful

To leave aside the complex particularities of the
different traditions may appear to reduce faith to a
bland, undifferentiated "glob." The richness of the
tradition, its color and texture, comes from the special
symbols in which its people have come to express their
laments and joys, their triumphs and tragedies, their
doubts and revelations. Particular doctrines and rites
have about them the smell of history. To step back
from all this may at first appear to step back into a
colorless abstraction. In fact it is to discover a world of
striking variety. To look at what goes into making a
person's faith is to discover a wide variety of styles,
styles of faithfulness of different quality, durability,
and sensitivity. It is a variety found within each tradition and cutting across all traditions. If comparisons are to be made between different faiths—this
way of looking at faith suggests—they will not be
comparisons of doctrine but comparisons of people's
ways of being faithful. They might include comparisons of the ways in which people relate to traditional
doctrine, the history of their coming to face life's ul-

timate issues, the range of experience that has gone into making their worldview, the tests that their ultimate trust has endured. And there are comparisons to be made.

In areas other than that of faith, researchers have long sought to get beneath the *what* of people's convictions in order to compare the *how* of their convictions, to put aside the different solutions that people hit upon in order to concentrate on the ways they approach the problem. Much of the research into children's knowledge of the physical world, for example, is of this kind—an investigation concerned not with *what* children know about the world but with *the way* they know. The what may well be different from one culture to another but there appear to be striking regularities in the way children reason, or rather, in the *ways* they reason, for apparently they regularly pass through a number of quite different ways of organizing their experience of the world. The focus here is not upon the content of the child's knowledge but on the processes of thinking that underlie the content.[4]

A similar investigation is under way in the area of moral judgment, one which concentrates not on the content of moral decisions but on the process by which people come to make their moral decisions: not on whether people are for or against abortion, for example, but on how they make up their minds. And again, in the passage from childhood to adulthood, it appears that people regularly pass through a number of quite different ways of making their moral decisions.[5] If you watch for the processes of thinking rather than the answers themselves, this research suggests, you are likely to find two things: first, that the processes are the same from one culture to another, and, second, that in the course of development people pass in a predictable order from one way of going about things to another.

Might the same not also be true of faith? It is beginning to look that way. Some early research in the area suggests that, despite the different words and symbols in which different people learn to think of the universe (and of their place and purpose within it), some important things can be said that are true of *all* these different expressions of faith. Despite the differences in *what* Catholics, Protestants, Jews, Muslims, and others believe, there are common patterns in their *ways of believing* whatever it is they believe. What is more, there appear to be common patterns in the *growth* of the faith of people who have been brought up in different traditions, an overall design in the manner in which different ways of believing succeed one another within the life of each believer.[6] If one looks past the different doctrines, in other words, what one finds is a number of ways of being faithful common to all traditions and a pattern of growing from one way to another that is also common to all traditions.

Stages of Faith

This research is one of the sources of "stage theory," the theory that people develop through childhood and on into adulthood by making a series of qualitative leaps, perhaps three or four major ones in the course of a lifetime, from one stage of development to another. Each stage means a consistent way of going about things, a way of coping with the world, a way of sorting out one's experience, a way of putting it all together in some satisfactory explanation. Depending on whether we are talking about the development of intellectual knowledge, moral reasoning, or faith, a stage will mean a consistent way of dealing with an intellectual problem, solving a moral dilemma, or dealing with life's ultimate questions. One way to deal with the physical world, for example, is on the basis of painstaking trial-and-error experimentation, the way a child does. Another is to spin out abstract theories in one's head, mentally weighing several different explanations of a problem. They represent different stages of intellectual development. One way to solve a moral dilemma is on the basis of personal friendship and loyalty. Another is impartially to balance the rights of everybody involved. They are different stages of moral development. One way to make sense of life's largest questions is to trust the wisdom of a respected religious authority. Another is to struggle personally for the answers that are verified by one's own experience. They are different stages of faith development.

There are a number of standard images of human development. One favors the idea of development as an inner process. It is the image of the growing plant, all its potential contained within and blossoming forth in the natural course of events. Another emphasizes the role of external factors in development. The person is more like soft putty, shaped by the repeated touch of persons and events. The image we are working with here is not really weighted toward the individual *or* the environment: it is an image of growth in which all the action happens as the individual *confronts* the world as one continually trying to make sense of it and as the world continually confronts the individual as a problem to be solved. We develop by having constantly to deal with our environment, struggling all the time to keep a balance between our present way of making sense of things and the new information that keeps intruding upon our minds from outside. It is a give-and-take process. Sometimes the mind is able to take in the new information, making sense of it in terms of our existing patterns of interpretation. Sometimes the mind has to "give" a little in the face of the new information. Every problematic situation is likely to involve some pushing and tugging at our ways of making sense of what is going on, forcing us to adjust or "bend" our theories, pressing us to make explicit what was previously only implicit in them. And occasionally we find ourselves inadequate to the challenge.

As long as we are open to experience we will be periodically pressed against the limits of our mind. New experience outgrows the old explanations. Old authorities turn out to have clay feet. We get caught up in contradictions, baffled by the unresolvable dilemma. Rock-bottom assumptions are overturned. We can't make sense of things any more. It doesn't happen often but, when it does, it means crisis. Sometimes we will shut out the new experience and withdraw to the safety of our former innocence. But if we resolve our distress creatively it will be by hitting on a fundamentally new way of making sense of the world, a way that is able to include the new experience in an expanded, better informed, more durable way of looking at things. That kind of radical reorganization of our mind and reorganization of our lives, as distinct from the day-to-day adjustments made without any great upheaval, signals the passage from one stage of development to the next.[7]

Note that there is a certain logic in passing from one stage to another. When we face one of these turning-

points and successfully negotiate it, it is because we
need to. It is because we are left with no other choice,
short of blocking out what we can no longer block out
with any honesty. If we pass to a new way of interpreting the world it is because the new way can account
for things that the old way no longer could. We are
now able to acknowledge considerations previously
ignored, to account better for all the facts, to embrace
a wider range of perspectives. We couldn't have
reached the new stage without having first passed
through the former stage. But the new one is not
simply different; it is better.[8]

Toward the Broader Vision

From the very way in which people are said to develop, it should be apparent that each subsequent
stage of development will be distinguished from the
previous one by a certain expansiveness, a moving
outward, a broadening of vision and concern. The
journey outward begins with the self-centeredness of
the very young. In the uncomplicated world of infancy, infants need attend only to their own needs and
interpret the world only from their own point of view.
Growing up means having to take account of a wider
and wider world, one which comes to include many
other people's needs and many other points of view.
An important part of this process is the natural argu-
ing among children that creates unrest in their minds
by presenting angles on a problem that they cannot
satisfactorily deal with in terms of their present way
of thinking. This is a challenge to self-centered thinking, pressing the child gradually to adjust his or her
perspective on things in order to coordinate it with
the perspectives of others.[9]

Growth is marked by expanding role-taking ability, that is, the growing capacity to take the point of view of others. At the early, self-centered stages there is at best a pragmatic acknowledgment of other people's needs. This changes as the child learns to "get inside another's head," to take people's inner motivation into account, to feel with and for the other. With further growth, empathy is extended beyond those near and familiar to us to those whom we come to recognize as sharing the life and fortunes of our societal group and, eventually, to those whose only link with us is that of our shared humanity.[10]

In very general terms, the developmental journey begins as we emerge from the relatively unfettered consciousness of the infant, where fantasy can run free and no demands beyond the self need to be acknowledged. The world will soon begin to impose its order on us. For one thing, it is a world inhabited by other selves with their own needs. We learn the inevitable negotiations and trade-offs. As we learn to see beneath the surfaces of other faces we discover a world of feelings—affection, trusting, hurting—and face the new challenges and restraints of love and loyalty. As experience takes us beyond the interpersonal world of family and friends, we encounter the yet wider order of society, urging us to submit to the wisdom of its authorities and the discipline of its rules and teaching us the meaning of duty. An inner experience is likely to tug at us next, pressing against society's restraints and pitching us into a new struggle for the self, now self-aware and critical. If we ever move beyond that point, it will be to win a new peace with the world, a world peopled now not simply with rivals, friends, fellow-citizens, or fellow-rebels, but with fellow human beings credited with the same dignity and enjoying the same rights as ourselves.[11]

The image of growth here is one of scales falling from our eyes, of expanded vision, of deliverance from the naive point of view. Growing essentially means growing wiser, more conscious of our limits and more sensitive to the claims of others. This can happen only as we become more self-conscious of our own point of view, able to see that it is just that—a point of view —and not the whole picture. To achieve the wider perspective, we need to be able to take a step back, to win some distance on the view of things in which we have been embedded up till now. What seemed to be the whole story will then turn out to have been simply a part of the whole; what seemed to be the truth will turn out to have been simply an angle on the truth.

As long as we remain really open to dialogue with those whose experience differs from our own, we will be pressed to own up to the limits of our own vision but will come by the same token to a greater appreciation of the variety and richness of the whole picture. Less embedded in the prejudices of our own culture, we become readier for membership in a universal community of humankind. This is the broad picture that emerges of the way that persons mature. Where growing in faith is seen as an element of personal growth—its "depth dimension"—it will follow the same contours, ending in a faith that is not limited to the concerns of an individual or group but expressing the concerns and hopes of a universal human community.

A Vision of Justice

If faith grows as its field of vision and concern broadens, then it is not difficult to see that issues of social justice will emerge as the central problems with which a maturing faith will have to deal. Issues of social justice are essentially about who is to be cared for and who neglected, who is to be included in our community of concern and who excluded, whose point of view is to be taken seriously and whose ignored. As faith grows, it challenges all the established answers to these questions. It presses against the institutions that frame the established answers. It comes up against the political, social, and economic rules that protect the established answers. As it grows, faith necessarily comes to challenge the system that protects some while neglecting others. It cannot do otherwise once it comes to the point of really embracing the perspectives and concerns of the neglected.

Of course, faith may never get to that point of awareness. It may never grow beyond the concerns of a single individual or class of people. It may come to affect a universalist vision and mouth the slogans of peace and justice, but never really from any viewpoint other than its own. The point here is simply that the expanding awareness and concern that brings with it a genuine involvement in dismantling the oppressive society and creating in its place a community from which none is excluded is *the* measure of the maturing faith. Short of that, faith may be intensely preoccupied in a way that suggests serious piety, except that it is preoccupied with individualistic concerns. It may be moving in its sincerity, but nourished by a pathetically thin slice of human experience. It may yearn for a just and peaceful human community but be innocent of the social structures that thwart it.

In all of these cases, faith may yet have an integrity of its own. Development is an orderly process, not in the sense that it will not be marked by crises, chaos, and distress, but in the sense that there is a logical

progression in the crises and in the solutions we hit
upon to deal with them. One implication of this is
that each stage has its proper place in the scheme of
things. It may not be the most mature stage but it
may yet be the most appropriate, for the appropriate
stage is the one that fits logically at a given point in a
person's life-history.[12] At the same time, to have a
sense of the whole process of development is to have a
standard against which to measure particular ways
of being faithful. Where the most mature faithfulness
is seen as the most-embracing, less-embracing forms
of faith can be seen for what they are, less mature
stages along the way.[13]

From the point of view of the dynamics of faith
development, the key to faith's quality is its *awareness*, not merely its good will, sincerity, or energy, but
its breadth. This is not to take the virtue out of faith,
as if faith were to be judged on its knowledgeability or
its social planning—a case, as somebody once remarked, of "dreaming of systems so perfect that no
one will need to be good." But it is to recognize that
the level of our awareness is integral to the quality of
our care. The awareness that characterizes the mature faith has nothing to do with scientific expertise
or technical competence. Rather, it is a measure of the
range of voices we have learned to listen to, the range
of concerns we are able to feel for, the range of people
with whose experience we can identify. It is no glib
sophistication but a weathering hard won by experience. The developmental model does not drop
the virtue out of awareness. Nor does it permit
us to drop the awareness out of virtue. For, if that
happens, we are helpless to judge among the varieties of faith, bound to give equal value to every
sincere expression, none having anything to recom-

mend it or distinguish it from others except the intensity of its commitment. Or, failing that, we are thrown
back on yet another criterion—this one owing nothing
either to breadth of awareness *or* intensity of
commitment—namely, blind obedience to the received tradition. The course of faith's development
provides us with a better yardstick.

A Changing Chorus

With the help of that yardstick it becomes possible
to begin an assessment of some of the shifts and con-
flicts that have shaken the church in recent years.
Upheavals are as old as the church itself and recent
years have been especially turbulent. Modern Protestant and Jewish communities have been profoundly
affected by the liberalism that arose in the late
nineteenth century. For Roman Catholics, the Second
Vatican Council stands out as the watershed of recent
times. In all these changes, what is essentially at
stake is the definition of holiness.

There are, of course, other issues—questions of
the church's mission, authority, orthodoxy, ethical
standards—but they all come down finally to the
question of what it means to be holy. What image are
we to have of the ultimately faithful person? The
answer to that question is going to look quite different
to people at different stages in the development of
their faith. For one of the things that is meant by
being at a particular faith stage is that being faithful
will take on a particular significance, make a particular set of demands, require a particular kind of response. What it means to be faithful depends on what
stage a person is coming from. People at different
stages can be expected to struggle for their own defi-

nition, and to see their own definition officially recognized.

In this light, the identification of faith with orthodoxy—conformity to the officially-defined beliefs—appears as one way of being faithful, one way of defining holiness. It represents a particular stage of faith, the stage institutionalized in pre-Vatican II Catholicism. Characteristically, faith focuses at this stage on the faith community's established formulations of doctrine. Status belongs primarily to those charged with guarding the tradition and preserving its meaning intact. The main argument for retaining Latin as the church's official language, we recall, was that, as an unchanging language, it was the vehicle best suited for this task. For the faithful, piety is defined primarily in terms of a trusting obedience. The shape of the community is the pyramid, its members arranged in a hierarchy, bound by relations of authority and dependence and addressed in the language of parent and child. Direct instruction is the favored method of education, a method described by exiled Brazilian educator Paulo Freire as the "banking" method.[14] Indeed, the language of the banking world strongly flavored the catechesis of the period: faith was referred to as a deposit, with an emphasis on its security; the bank itself was relied on to define the value of the deposit and the rules for protecting the investment; the appropriate attitude of the institution's clientele was one of trust.

Certainly, the general attitude of conformity characteristic of this stage of faith allowed for some variations. Some stressed the importance of an affective commitment, following the preference of *The Imitation of Christ* for feeling compunction rather than being able to define it. Educated Catholics, on the other hand, often professed a sturdily intellectual faith. They valued the keen-witted apologists who publicly defended the church's doctrines. Many will recall their Catholic high-school education as a kind of basic combat training aimed at arming its students with iron-clad answers to all the questions likely to be raised by a hostile, faithless world. They would be able on occasion to direct stinging criticism at that world's conventional wisdom, but not at the church's own conventions. *They* were beyond question. When it came to the tradition itself, Catholics submitted their critical faculties. For that submission, after all, was what faith was about.

It was a model of fidelity that worked best in relatively unselfcritical times, when it was easier than it is now to believe that we possessed *the* truth because our religious ancestors had happily been granted the revelation by God. But a wave of scholarship would puncture that confidence. Literary critics, historians, sociologists, and anthropologists would instruct us in the limits of revelation, making us sensitive to the historical circumstances, vested interests, and human frailties that limit every perception of the truth and condition its every formulation. Any truth, we would discover, is one truth among others. We would learn modesty in making our own claims, and tolerance for the claims of others.

Tolerance for the claims of others is not the same as the belief that one claim is as good as another. But, historically, it proved a short step from tolerance to relativism. In the new climate the old doctrines were no longer sacrosanct, the old authorities no longer able to exact the same allegiance. No truth need be recognized now except "being true to yourself," no injunction absolute except "to do your own thing."

Where the old piety meant obedience, the new piety would come to mean authenticity. What had emerged was a fundamentally different way of being faithful, a new faith stage.

Into the composition of faith there entered a new element, a consciousness of self. The paternalism of the old hierarchy would be no longer tolerated, as believers struggled to be recognized as adults and dealt with as equals. Especially for many low-ranking clerics, members of religious orders, and lay people, the spread of the new fidelity signaled a heady new realignment with traditional superiors and established truths. It accounted for much of Vatican II's sense of excitement and deliverance. It meant space to criticize the tradition and the right to measure the received wisdom against one's own unique experience. Where the glory of the old theology had been its very antiquity, people spoke openly now of the *new* theology. Soft on the old certitudes, it would pay special attention to the self, opening a dialogue with psychology and yielding new insights into the relationship between faith and identity, between Christian maturity and self-actualization, between holiness and wholeness.

Religious education would find a new method, too, premised less on the sanctity of external norms than on trust in the unfolding of the child's inner potential. The new catechesis would be client-centered, its truths blander, less concerned with banking a deposit of doctrine than with nurturing the growing plant. For the realization of the self was now what faith was about.

The faith that celebrates the fulfillment of the self represents a development beyond one that binds the self in childlike dependence. To many it has meant liberation from authoritarian bondage. Faith has become a celebration of our freedom. Yet it is sobering to realize that for the vast masses of the world's people our new faith is worse than irrelevant, as long as the energies that might free them are still channelled into the celebration of our own deliverance. If we are to be sensitized to the limits of our contemporary forms of fidelity, we will need a sharper image of what a truly developed faith entails than the image for which we have generally settled. This is one of the promises of the attention being newly paid to the dynamics of faith's development. But perhaps the greatest benefit we stand to gain is a renewed respect for *truth*.

In freeing us from the tyranny of the old certitudes, relativism has served many of us well. Years ago, Oscar Hammerstein posed the problem eloquently. "Too many people," he commented, "become certain of too many things too early in their lives. They lack the wisdom and the courage to expose their ideas to healthy doubts. They cling with blind passion to their false certainties and, too often, they are ready to kill or be killed for them. In these absolutists lies the seed of tragedy. The earth is sick with them." Many of us heard an indictment of the church in words like that, and we responded with a fervent "Amen." How much blood had been shed in the name of truth, how much freedom denied in maintaining the superiority of "our" truths over "their" truths, how much hostility in defense of the one true faith! Where the quest for truth meant comparing our truths with their truths—along the lines that Christianity is truer than Islam, Catholicism truer than Protestantism, and so on—better that the quest for truth be abandoned. Better simply to affirm that nobody's truth is

truer than anybody else's. We settled into an easy
ecumenism and enjoyed the leisure to experiment,
each to shape a truth for ourselves. And yet the earth
is still sick.

A Faith to Press the Harder Questions

One thing is clear: in the relativism that has cleared
for us a space in which to develop there is nothing to
press on us the hardest questions, nothing to press on
us the question of other people's development or the
question of how our development may be linked to
their failure to develop. Raising issues like that sup-
poses a new concern for truth.

Where faith is extricated from the doctrines in
which it comes to expression, it allows for a different
kind of comparison, not along the lines that Christian
truths are superior to Islamic truths, but along the
lines that, whether one is Christian or Muslim, some
ways of being Christian or Muslim are better than
other ways. Not merely better but truer. Better because truer. For the understanding of the process of
faith's development carries its own implications for
truth. Where faith is seen to develop as it comes to
embrace a wider range of perspectives and to include
the concerns of a wider community, the more developed faith is the truer faith. Truer because including more angles on the truth. Truer because including
more people's experience of the truth. The truest
faith, then, is the faith that embraces the perspectives and celebrates the hopes of the whole human
community.

The search for such a faith cannot help but press
upon us the questions of how our development relates
to other people's failure to develop; it cannot help but

bring us up against the political, economic, and social structures that protect the advantaged while neglecting the disadvantaged; it cannot help but challenge us to dismantle the structures of oppression and to remake the world in justice. What we are able to learn from attending to the process of faith's development is what Jews and Christians have inherited from their tradition: an appreciation of the truth that sets peoples free. What is symbolized in the one instance by the loving concern of the one and only God is seen in the other as the logical culmination of our development as faithful human beings. The failure that the religious tradition describes as a refusal to worship the living God appears in the literature of development as a breakdown in the process of growth. From each source we learn that there is nothing arbitrary about the meaning of mature faith. It will be known by its works. And its works are the works of justice.

CHAPTER 3

How Faith Gets Sidetracked

The Power of the (Religious) Idea

It is inscribed upon a clockface somewhere—the railway station at South Bend comes into mind—*Nothing is as powerful as an idea whose time has come.* Though not an exclusively American faith, it surely has some important roots among this nation's first European settlers. Putting tyranny behind them, they were bent on building a new society just as good as their power to envision it. The quality of the new order would be measured by the quality of the ideas that went into designing it. Could it be any other way? For what determines the quality of the societies we build if not the quality of the dreams we dream? What challenges us to create something better if not our ability to imagine something better? What makes us critical of the way things are if not our ability to envisage the way things ought to be? Once imagination withers we learn to accept the existing state of affairs; once our dreams fade we mistake mere facts for reality.

Religion has traditionally offered to rescue us from our submission to mere facts. Its sense of an *ultimate* reality ("that eye hath not seen nor ear heard") fires the imagination, calling our attention to an order of things much vaster than what meets the eye. It warns us against jumping to conclusions about the way things are, against taking the facts too seriously. The religious impulse is one of transcendence, pressing us toward the reality that lies beyond the obvious. It enables us to see the present state of affairs as always provisional, under the judgment of what is yet to come. Should we lose the religious impulse we come to accept the obvious as the ultimate. We learn to live with the facts. If the world is oppressive and greedy, that's "just the way it is." We come to terms with it. Losing our thirst for God, we settle for some idol. But, as long as we remain open to it, our religious longing continually upsets our complacency, challenges our easy truths, startles us with insight; it exposes our petty-mindedness, our cowardice, our easy submission to the world's brutality; it nurtures visions of the good society more profound than any we might otherwise conceive. That, at any rate, is its promise.

It is a promise that faith can change the world. And it is a promise that rests on the power of the idea—especially the religious idea—to challenge the old order and create the new. Our social strategies are, after all, only as good as the purposes we have in mind. Whether our programs are capitalist, socialist, or of some other design, we are ever in danger of becoming victims of our mean and tawdry images of the good society. This is why we need religion: relentlessly to question our purposes and to enlarge our visions. If justice is to be done, it must be adequately envisaged. If only it is adequately envisaged, we insist on hoping, justice will be done.

If the recent study of faith's development links mature faith to the works of justice, it is because the maturity of one's faith is linked there to the adequacy of one's vision. The maturing of faith is seen as an expansion of the mind, faith's transforming power flowing from those revolutions in consciousness that mark the stages of its development. It is the vision —the quality of our thinking—that counts. Should a faith emerge with the power to challenge the racist, greedy, and violent society, it will be the fruit of a vision that has expanded to embrace interests beyond those of the individual or group to encompass those of a universal human community. It is the possibility of thinking more and more broadly that opens the way to a more and more inclusive human community, a more and more just society. It is an altogether exciting prospect, a bold interpretation of the path of faith's development, an analysis full of the promise of justice. But beneath this analysis of faith, we should not forget, there lies another faith: that is, faith in the power of the idea, faith in the ability of cultivated minds to make a difference.

The Liberal Vision

Linking the maturity and effectiveness of faith with breadth and sensitivity of vision has come from that particular current of cultivated thinking that is usually termed the liberal tradition. It springs from a long tradition of faith in the power of the idea; but breadth and sensitivity of vision are its special claims to distinction. Liberalism is the editorial page of the *New York Times*. It prides itself on its openness to all sides of an issue, its sensitivity to different viewpoints, its balance. But the essence of the liberal faith is that progress toward the good society rests on the free play of ideas. It celebrates breadth over narrowness, knowledge over ignorance, openmindedness

over dogmatism, calm statement over strident asser-
tion, tolerance over redneck prejudice. Always grist
for its mill are issues of conscience, and nothing
arouses the liberal conscience more than injustice. It
is not the only faith to have inspired the nation, of
course, but it has frequently been the faith of the
educated. For it is above all a faith *in* education—
a faith in the ability of education to broaden the mind
and in the ability of the broadminded to work things
out rationally and peaceably.

Nor has liberalism bypassed the churches. By the
end of the liberal sixties many of our newer catechisms well reflected the temper of the times. They
were broad in their vision and sensitive to issues of
justice. They contained graphic pictures of hungry
and war-torn peoples from around the world. The
filmstrips designed for the parents of children about
to be baptized focused on the struggle for civil rights
as a test of the Christian life. The newer anthologies
included hymns to universal community. Parishes
began to form "peace and justice" committees and
study groups on Vietnam, racism, and corporate
power. In all of this there appears the strength of the
liberal vision, its concern for justice as the responsibility of any educated mind, its emphasis on progressive education as the path of justice.

A Vision of the Just Society

This, too, is the strength of the liberal interpretation of the growth of faith, the promise contained in
linking the development of faith with a broadening of
the mind. For one thing, it guarantees that justice
will be recognized as a central issue for the mature
believer. It points up the limits of all individualistic
images of faithfulness—whether Christian holiness is

seen as the flowering of one's personal potential, as unlocking the secret of inner peace, or even as accepting Jesus as one's personal Lord and Savior. Faith is rescued from preoccupation with individual salvation or self-development. Delivered from merely private concerns, it is made available for the concerns of society.

Obvious to the liberal sensibility is that injustice is a challenge to faith and that injustice is a social reality. The oppression that shackles the lives of two out of every three persons is built into the social structures that link together the peoples of the world. Oppression is a product of the rules we all live by. They are the rules that govern access to power and resources, the ability to trade, the planning of public policy, the allocation of prestige, the right to make decisions. The rules are advantageous to the lucky few, disadvantageous to many, and remarkably consistent. The development of a faith with real implications for justice will necessarily have to come to grips with these rules and with the social structures that embody them. The liberal account of faith has taken note of these things and, though it has survived only precariously in the parish life of the more quiescent seventies, it remains compelling. What bears closer scrutiny is the faith that *underlies* the religious faith of liberals: faith in the power of the idea, more particularly, faith in the power of liberal thinking to bring about the just society.

Idea and Reality

Though not always fashionable, praising the idea of justice is notoriously easy. Creating the reality of justice is another matter. It is not that praising the idea is a bad thing: minds that are capable of wres-

tling with the idea of justice are no doubt more en-
riched than minds never stirred by such a concern.
Wrestling with the idea may even be the prelude to
creating the reality. On that point, however, we
should not be overly optimistic. For, while the idea of
justice may involve a change of consciousness, the
reality will involve a change of society. And changes
in our minds need not wait upon changes in the world.

This distinction is critical. It will matter little if, as
the mind grows and the visions expand, the social
structure itself remains unchanged. If we do not take
hold of the reality of justice it will matter little that
we have taken hold of the idea. Accordingly, if we are
concerned with the question of how the development
of faith connects with the *reality* of the just society
we will not be dazzled simply by the nobility of
faith's ideals or the grandeur of its visions. What
matters—it is there that people's lives are actually
crushed or cherished—is the social arrangement that
designates for each of us our place, our worth, and our
chances. Even though the liberal model of holiness
brings to the fore issues of justice neglected by individualistic models, its chances of effecting real social
change remain tenuous as long as it rests that hope
solely on change in people's hearts and minds.

It is tempting to think that there is no real problem
here. It may seem obvious that the idea will lead to
the reality, that changes in society will follow upon
changes in people's thinking, that the kingdom of God
names a reign in our hearts and minds *before* it names
the social and political mesh of our lives together. But
does it really follow that, as the scales fall from our
eyes, the chains fall from the oppressed? Alas, it is
not necessarily the case, and history gives us scant
reason to count on it.

Grappling intellectually with issues of justice has,

for the restless mind, its own dynamism and its own rewards. The issues are "out there" for any open mind to see. They press on sensitive consciences. They raise troubling questions, questions that will not go away. They make us uneasy, forcing us to grapple with them, to be able to deal with them. We are pressed to "take a position" on the vexing social dilemmas of our day lest we be tripped up by our prejudices or caught in our insensitivities. And, especially if we have the benefit of a liberal education, we may indeed learn to cope with the day's injustices. We may learn to anticipate all angry accusations, turning them aside with disarming candor. We may learn to soften the cry of distress with gently-couched compassion. When once we have heard it all we will be better prepared, less likely to be taken unawares, less likely to put a liberal foot wrong. Even though the cities burn, we may yet learn to keep our cool.

Should this seem too cynical, it is well to remember that an extensive and well-funded industry—the knowledge industry—exists in large part to provide the necessary skills for dealing intellectually with the world's pain. The main problem is not that our colleges, classrooms, libraries, and study circles fail to acknowledge the justice issues. In liberal circles at any rate, our course lists and bookshelves are filled with discussion of these themes. But that is precisely the problem: while the situation cries out for action we continue the endless round of discussion, all the time convinced that in our wordy concern we are really addressing the issues. We are not. We are avoiding them. Our failure to take the kind of action that might change an oppressive situation results less from any failure to consider the oppression or to be concerned about it than from our uncanny ability to keep channeling our outrage into a flow of words.

From Anguish to Action

Where faith is thought of as a purely private endowment, growth in holiness takes one along a wholly interior path, the individual walking alone before God. One responds to the neighbor as another individual called to take the same inner journey. The image is of a world of people summoned individually to make the commitment of faith and supporting one another in the personal commitment each has made. Social, political, and economic structures are not a part of the picture. The world's evil is the result of sin in the individual heart and will be resolved only as individual hearts find salvation. The liberal account of faith claims something more than this, linking growth in faith with the growing ability to identify with different groups of people, to see things from their perspectives, and so to get a sense of the whole framework linking the fortunes of one to the misfortunes of the other. Faith becomes aware of social structure and of structured sin. It is for this reason that the critical issues for the mature believer are not simply issues of individual salvation but issues of social justice, issues of fairness in the social, economic, and political structures framing the lives of the world's peoples. According to the liberal account, the journey of faith will inevitably bring the believer up against all the cozy arrangements that embrace the favored but dismiss the rest as beyond the pale.

It is important to recognize, however, that at this point even the believer sensitive to injustice will still have a choice. One response, of course, is to take action to dismantle the oppressive social structures. But other alternatives exist. Failing action, there remain discussion, concern, even anguish. Failing action, there is still "consciousness-raising." But, failing action, there is no real change. While barriers may tumble in the mind, the social barriers that divide the world's people will stand as securely as ever. The energy of faith, the brilliance of its visions, the power of its ideals: all will have been routed down the path of inner transformation, channelled into a spiritual odyssey with implications—perhaps important implications—for the believer, but without importance for society. Universal community turns out in this case to be a state of mind, and the struggle for justice another head trip.[1]

Bringing faith to bear on issues of justice is already an achievement; for those of liberal sensibilities, it is an important achievement; but it is not the achievement of justice. A more difficult, and more important, task lies ahead: to free faith's concern from the arena of ideas, good intentions, and moral anguish, and to translate it into effective action.

The Action that Changes Society

The question that all this raises for the way we think of the growth of faith is this: should the maturity of faith be gauged by our ideas or our action, by the changes that come about in our minds or the changes we bring about in our society? As long as the ideas and the actions are thought to "go together," of course, the question seems frivolous. But the proven tendency we have to postpone the action while we continue to explore the ideas suggests that the question is an important one. And the answer to it seems clear. As long as growing in faith implies bringing about the just society *as a reality* then, at some point, faith will be said to grow only as it results in action to transform the social structures of injustice. The sign of faith's maturing will be not simply the changes it fosters in the mind but the changes it fosters in society. At the point that this transforming action becomes the test for faith any merely mental response will be seen for what it is: a siphoning-off of faith's energy, a diversion of its power, a sidetrack.[2]

It would be foolish to deny that ideas have frequently played a critical role in history or that words themselves sometimes constitute bold and decisive action. Letters written by Paul to the fledgling Christian communities, the sharply contested phrasing of the Nicene Creed, the Great Charter of rights signed by King John at Runnymede, the ninety-five theses nailed to a church door at Wittenberg, the U.S. Constitution, the Communist Manifesto, the documents of Vatican II—all have shaped the future course of events, some for centuries to follow. Not all words are matched by action, however, and not all actions are actions for social justice. In fact, if it comes down to the likelihood of words actually *changing* anything, ringing declarations about justice are as likely as any to vanish into thin air.

This is not to suggest that there is necessarily anything sinister or hypocritical about the gap between rhetoric and action. There seems to be at work here some dynamic deeper than moral cowardice. Whether ideas and words about justice are consistently accompanied by effective action appears to depend on one factor more than any other: namely, on *whose* ideas and words they are, on where they come to take root, and especially on whether the people doing the thinking and talking have a real "gut" interest in the outcome. Having an intellectual or moral concern about justice is one thing; having your life at stake is another. The main difference is likely to lie in how urgent it seems that stirring ideas be matched with effective action. Surely there is a clue here as to why ideas—even those which (their time having long since come) are reputed to be so powerful—so rarely deliver on what they promise.

One measure of the ability of a nation to provide for its people what they need for a decent life is termed by economists its per capita gross national product. It stands for the total value of the goods and services produced by a nation, divided by the number of its people. In the United States, it presently stands at something more than $7000. For 65 percent of the world's people, living mainly in Asia and Africa, it amounts to less than $1000. For 29 percent of the people it comes to less than $200. These figures have an immediate bearing on a matter of fundamental importance to people—their chance of staying alive. While the United States, West Germany, Japan, France, and the United Kingdom can expect no more than 20 infant deaths per thousand live births, countries like Ethiopia, Bangladesh, Indonesia, Pakistan, Nigeria, and Egypt can expect from 121 to 180. While in the rich countries one can expect to live for over seventy years, in the poor countries life expectancy runs at between forty and fifty years.[3]

This is the state of the world in which ideas and words, including ideas and words about justice, are bandied about. It is important to realize that ideas do not exist in a vacuum, floating on some ethereal plane above history and enjoying a power of their own. They are the ideas of people, thrown by accident of birth into a particular point in history and into a particular place on the structure of the world's wealth and power. Ideas live among people moved by different gut concerns, having different agendas and priorities, having different stakes in the existing social arrangement and, accordingly, having different stakes in real social change. People's real interests run deeper than the ideas that claim their conscious attention. The ideas that seem at first glance to be what makes the world go around may be in fact at the service of more fundamental concerns.

What You See Depends on Where You Stand

Traditionally, not all classes of people have enjoyed the same freedom to traffic in ideas. This social role is given to the intellectuals—the professional thinkers, artists, writers, researchers, and teachers. These are the mind-shapers, the opinion-makers, the arbiters of taste and judgment. They certify the credentials of those who claim to be educated, and education is the badge of membership in their company. They are the guardians of a nation's culture, the interpreters of its inherited wisdom, the keepers of its ideals. As far as the distribution of the world's prestige and rewards is concerned, they are a relatively privileged group. To do their creative tasks they are freed by the labor of manual workers from the monotonous tasks of production and financially supported by governments, corporations, foundations, and the patronage of the wealthy.

Many intellectuals are frankly involved in explaining the social system, justifying it in terms of the traditional values of the culture and ferreting out the facts it needs to operate. Others are skilled in critical reflection on society and in weighing the merits of alternate social structures. But all of them are advantaged by the existing system, dependent on it for the freedom to do what they do best, and indebted to it, even if they are sensitive to its inequities. Where their thinking leads to action it is not likely to be the kind of action that would threaten the social structure on which they depend. Where their thinking *is* critical of the very social structure it is not likely to lead to action.

This is not to suggest that the educated are corrupt or insensitive to injustice. It *is* to suggest that where we stand on the social hierarchy necessarily gives us our point of view, our perspective on things. From where we stand we get a certain impression of the social landscape—a sense of what is right, sensible, urgent, desirable, and dangerous. Not least, we get a sense of the worth of the social hierarchy itself. If the creativity and ideas of the intellectuals and artists—the people charged in our society with the tasks of thinking, teaching, writing, sculpting, painting, acting, philosophizing, justifying, extolling, questioning, and condemning—do not lead to the kind of action that would change the social structure, it is hardly coincidental that these people are generally favored by that structure. That is not a moral judgment; it is simply a fact about society. How the situation looks to us depends inevitably on where we stand. We have no other vantage-point.[4]

Education introduces us to the company of the intellectuals. It is above all a company of people who trust in the value of ideas. They are often among those most committed to social progress, and even to social justice. Their sincerity is not at issue here. But if, as a matter of social fact, they stand among the advantaged, that fact will certainly make a difference to the way they see things. What is taken for progress and what looks like justice will reflect the particular view one gets from the lofty world of liberal arts and education.

Living in the world of ideas is, in both senses of the word, a heady existence. It is exciting to be caught up in the continuing exchange of ideas, to tackle anew the perennial problems of human existence, to guide students as they press up against their own intellectual frontiers. For the ethically sensitive, it is satisfying to put one's mind to stubborn social issues, to capture on canvas a people's suffering, to publish brilliant exposés of injustice, to call the nation back to its ideals. In general, things appear to be moving. Idea follows idea; book follows book; argument follows argument. It is easy to believe that progress is being made, that the real state of affairs is changing. Especially if they are ideas, books, and arguments about justice, it is easy to believe that they are making the world more just. It is easy to believe that good ideas must make a difference. It is only from a different perspective that things are seen to remain mostly the same, good ideas or not. Only from the perspective of the disadvantaged does the gap between good idea and real change seem wide and obvious. Only from that perspective, of course, is real change a real-life issue.

Whether justice is done depends finally on whether people take action to change the structures of injustice. Whether ideas about justice are matched by action is not something that can be predicted just by looking at the ideas themselves. It is more telling to look at the people among whom the ideas are stirring, to look at the life-chances afforded them by the existing social system and, accordingly, the real interest they have in changing it. Long schooling at the hands of the powerful may make it difficult at first for oppressed people to identify, articulate, or trust their own ideas, and even then the legislatures, courts, and guns of the powerful may keep them from acting on what they see. But, when action alone can make a difference to their lives, they are unlikely to settle, as the advantaged do so easily, for heady discussion, concerned handwringing, or anguished art.

The connection between thinking and action that seems so obvious to the liberal intellectual is quickly recognized as illusory by those who have so often heard the rhetoric of justice and so rarely felt any change in their situation. Precisely because they have seen the two so frequently sundered, the linking of reflection and action is for the oppressed a theme of central importance. The hungry cannot afford to place too much trust in the free flow of liberal ideas about the just society when the only thing that will fill their bellies is the action that will restore to them their share of the land and its produce. When it comes down to action, different perspectives yield quite different imperatives. How urgent it seems that ideas be matched by action is related to how closely one's life-chances depend on it.

It is easy for us to trust in the power of ideas to bring about a more just world if we overlook the thinker's point of view. It is easy to trust in broadminded, ethically sensitive leadership from the top if we ignore the inherent limits of the view from the top. Doing justice then appears primarily as an intellectual or moral issue, a matter of wisdom, intent, and perseverance. Good leaders make good decisions, just leaders just decisions. If injustice persists, it will be remedied by putting at the top people of broader vision and stronger principle. But it doesn't work. The almost uncanny impotence of this wise and sensitive leadership actually to change the conditions that oppress people cannot be adequately explained as a failure of intelligence or moral nerve on the part of those at the top. Rather, it is leadership from the top that is itself the problem.

Injustice persists because responsibility for deciding the use of the world's resources, and for justifying those decisions, rests with people who are advantaged by the present social arrangement. The problem lies in the system that gives to some people the right to make decisions for others, that gives to the favored the right to make decisions for all. Except where the exercise of power is openly cynical it is generally hoped that the intelligence and good will of the decision-makers will make up for any gap separating their experience and point of view from the experience and point of view of those whose lives their decisions will affect. That hope is not justified. To women, peoples in the poor nations, and peoples of color it does not seem coincidental to their oppression that the decisions that affect them have been traditionally in the hands of First World, white males. Because the problem is one of perspective rather than one of moral character it will be resolved only by changing the way decisions get made and not simply by staffing the process with well-meaning people. The alternative is for decisions to be made by the people who stand to be affected by them.

On Real Broadmindedness

If we are to hope realistically in education—in broadening the mind—as the path to justice, we will need to be clear on the different meanings that broadening the mind can have. For people given a progressive education and accustomed to looking at issues "from every angle" it is easy to feel that they have passed beyond the limits of their inherited point of view. Is not this what is meant, after all, by the victory of tolerance over prejudice, balance over onesidedness, humanitarian benevolence over parochial narrowness? No doubt that does represent a broadening of sorts. However, there are limits to even the most liberal broadmindedness that the broadminded themselves cannot see, for they are visible only from another perspective. From the perspective of those whose opinions are never sought and whose ideas are never held in any regard, what is the worth of the liberal's expansive vision? It is certainly not broad enough to embrace *their* view of things. If the liberal thinks it is, so much the worse for the liberal. And, of course, so much the worse for the poor. To the poor, it has proved no blessing to have their lives charted by people who think they understand their problems. It is not liberal decision-makers they need but a chance to get in on making the decisions themselves.

Now, if we're going to talk about breadth of vision, *there* is a definition of breadth that would really mean a change. There is all the difference in the world between breadth as an embellishment of the liberal mind and breadth as a measure of whose interests have actually been consulted. Bringing the poor into the picture as people whose ideas and experience have to be heeded when the decisions are being made is to bring in people who cannot afford to settle for the vision of justice but only for the action that brings it about. In this sense, but only in this sense, do we have reason to hope that the broader vision will bridge the gap between reflection and action. Only when thinking is broadened by the participation of the poor and fired by their imperatives is a link reliably forged between the idea of justice and the struggle for its realization.

Nor is this simply a matter of action "flowing from" broader or more sensitive thinking. Rather, action proves in this case to be a *condition* of the broader thinking. The world is already set up to provide a liberal education for its elites; it is decidedly not set up to bring ordinary people into the company of those whose ideas have either to be heard or taken seriously. Simply to include as equal participants in the decision-making process those left out of account in the present reckoning would imply a fundamental social transformation. In this sense, but again only in this sense, is broader thinking inseparable from the action that actually changes the world. And only in this sense is it really relevant for justice. The measure of freedom for the oppressed is neither the expansiveness of the ideas that excite the educated nor the sincerity of those who have traditionally inherited society's leadership roles. The measure of their freedom is the action that undoes the social structure that values the thinking and leadership of the world's favored minority and restores those roles to all whose lives are at stake.

Thinking About God

In our society, thinking about God has not escaped the fate of thinking in general. In the hands of professionals, theology has served the social structure that frees them for their task. The gospel of a carpenter's son, spread by fishermen, shook the princes of church and state; reduced to a professional discipline, it became the ally and tool of princes. Again, it is not a matter of sincerity but of perspective and experience. Theology done by the privileged responds to the questions and concerns they are near enough to hear and feel. The ideas of justice and freedom are still proclaimed; still preserved are the gospel symbols of judgment, transcendence, eschaton, the kingdom of God. All that is missing is the input of oppressed peoples, their experience, questions, hopes, and concerns. These are the people among whom the gospel originally took root and who found in it words of life. But it has long come down to them filtered through an alien experience and shaped to serve other people's concerns. The gospel interpreted by those whose lives are valued by the social system is unlikely to challenge that system. Its mighty symbols are elevated to a plane of rhetoric safely removed from the earth's structured evils. Its inherent power is deflected from the work of social transformation, the moral energy of believers siphoned off into other tasks. For the oppressed, it is anything but good news.[5]

Many avenues lie open for the faith diverted from the task of social transformation. The theological discussion of justice can itself absorb much of the available energy and concern. And it will do so as long as it is responsive to a population whose needs are largely intellectual, whose questions are typically questions of "the meaning of life," and whose sense of meaning is threatened in a special way by their being privileged persons in a sea of misery.[6] Short of altering the objective situation, theologians will have their time cut out helping the comfortable make sense of it, helping them see their privilege in the context of God's overall providence.

Alternatively, energies deflected from dismantling

the social barriers that shut out the poor can be turned on the mental barriers that block out "unconscious vitality" or "cosmic consciousness." A parade of Vietnam-era activists illustrates, perhaps parodies, this diversion. Within a few short years of their confrontation with the political system they are found sitting at the feet of the Guru Maharaj-ji, dabbling in eastern mysticism, or exploring "altered states of consciousness." Nor is this development necessarily grotesque. Not only the passing activism of the sixties but the more enduring materialism of U.S. society leave deep inner hungers unsatisfied. Any renewal of society will be superficial, if not frightening, unless it also engages the individual soul and addresses its hungers. Inwardness is not itself the problem; the transformation of society will necessitate careful attention to the interior life. The problem lies in the separation of inner and outer transformation, often on the assumption that the one will "lead to" the other. But it is too often characteristic of those who find themselves favored by the existing social arrangement that the cultivation of their spiritual lives does little if anything to change it. Transcendental meditation may be much less destructive than the double martini before dinner; it may well help to alleviate the day's stresses; but it will do nothing of itself to alter the society that causes them.[7]

The arena of interpersonal relations provides another fashionable focus for faith's energies. Social issues are easily transposed to an interpersonal key, on the argument that justice begins at home. An Encounter weekend spent in reviving a marriage may do much to heal the abrasiveness and deceptions that creep into our relationships, scars that are frequently the legacy of society's brutal power plays. But postponing the healing of society for the sake of healing our personal wounds overlooks the fact that it is also society that inflicts the wounds. In that sense, the kingdom of God names a transformed social reality *before* it names a transformation in our hearts and minds. The piety that would reverse that order may help us to cope with the present system; it will not help us to change it. It *is* the piety of the system.

Among the most challenging and appealing examples of faith are to be found the lives of those who, short of changing the system, serve those who are broken by it. Mother Teresa of Calcutta typifies the ministry, and many could attest to the impressive courage and patience of persons nearer home working to restore lives that have been physically and emotionally shattered. Were such courage and patience our principal yardsticks of faith's development, people such as these would unquestionably illustrate its most mature forms. A faith that will carry the struggle to build the just society will certainly demand these qualities of dedication; but it will demand more. Beyond tending the victims of oppression, it will demand action to remedy the causes of oppression.

Theology of Liberation

With the post-war break-up of the old political empires, some voices began to be heard in the poor nations urging our missionaries to go home. At first it seemed to many an ungenerous response to years of missionary effort that we had long thought of as one of the most generous expressions of our faith. For many of us it was our first inkling of a vast gap in perspective that our good will had proven quite unable to bridge. Despite the fact that most of the former colonies have won their political independence, they remain locked in an economic empire dominated by the major world powers that systematically drains them of their resources and frustrates their development. Their experience of what it means to live, raise their families, and chart the course of their lives remains vastly different from our experience of these things. But their experience is more articulate now, their voices more insistent. For some years indigenous theologies have been developing, bringing the Gospel to bear on their experience, responsive to their questions, symbolizing their hopes, carrying as its core the theme of liberation.

For all our scholarship and idealism, it remains very difficult for us to hear without distortion these newly-raised voices of the poor. If we hear their message at all, it comes through with its urgency, its call for action, filtered out. The *conscientização* coined in the impoverished northeast of Brazil to describe a practical strategy for social change becomes our "consciousness-raising" and describes an intellectual exercise with consequences extending no further than our own hang-ups. The poor nations' theologies of liberation remain, however, the best hope we have of coming to appreciate the limits of even our best theological insights and our most generous ministries.

The Meaning of Maturity

There is an important clue here as to what breadth of vision and concern really entail. It is especially important for a model of faith development that takes universality as its yardstick, that takes a broadening awareness and concern as the sign of faith's maturing. What does it mean for faith that the awareness that is celebrated among the circles of the privileged may yet be abysmally unaware of the experience of most of the world's people, and that what appears to us as broadminded may appear to them as very parochial indeed? What does it mean for faith that what we so easily take for a fair and educated vision of the world so rarely demands that we actually do anything to change the structures that oppress people? It means that if growth in faith is to have any real connection with building the just society it will be measured not simply by the changes it yields in our minds but by the changes it yields in society, not simply by the quality of our thinking but by the effectiveness of our action.

The universality of its vision and concern may yet be taken as the central indicator of faith's maturity, but only if we are clear on what a more universal vision really entails. It will not be sufficient that our vision of the world has expanded as long as it remains *our* vision. It will not have expanded in any sense that would mark a real growth in faith unless *their* vision has been included. For only when our visions include the input of the oppressed will they be reliably tied to transforming action. Indeed, in a fundamental sense the divorce of vision and action will then have been resolved, for the inclusion of the wider range of people in our faithful reflection will already have entailed a transformation of the social structures that have traditionally locked their input out. Short of this, even the liberal faith fired with a vision of justice will have been shunted onto a sidetrack, still announcing its destination but in fact going nowhere.

CHAPTER 4

Faith and Community

The Company We Keep

"Conversion" once had a peculiar ring for Catholics. For one thing, it was something that Protestants did. Perhaps to marry a Catholic or following a series of instructions at the hands of some persuasive monsignor, a Protestant might "turn" and embrace Catholicism. That was conversion. It was not something that born Catholics expected to experience. In more recent times, happily, the word has regained something of its original, biblical meaning. Conversion means a profound inner transformation, a turning around, a radical change of heart. It is just as likely to mean recapturing the truth of one's own tradition as it is to mean switching to some different tradition. Any adult faith, moreover, will need to be shaken by the occasional conversion if it is not to stagnate.

Even so, conversion is still likely to be thought of as essentially an individual experience, like Saul's being stunned by the glory of the Lord on the road to Damascus. But it took more than a single private experience for Saul to become Paul. It took his mov-

69

ing, spiritually as well as geographically, beyond Tarsus. It took his finding a new people. It took his finding acceptance in the Christian community.[1] The challenge to Paul's former faith, and to the vision nurtured in his former community, would for the rest of his days come from his now being answerable to this wider community. His new vision and commitment would depend less on any private flash of inspiration than on the fact that he daily broke bread with Gentiles. Of course, it was his rich Jewish heritage that he would continue to draw on, its symbol of the one and only God that would still inspire him. If he found new meaning and new inspiration in the tradition, it was because he saw it now from a wider perspective, from the outsider's point of view.

There is a lesson in this about faith's journey, in particular about those leaps in consciousness that look like important milestones along the way. The lesson is that faith is a question not so much of the visions we have as of the company we keep. Or, a better way to put it perhaps, that the kind and quality of our visions—including their capacity to guide and sustain us in doing whatever it seems must be done —depends on the kind of people with whom we interact. Behind any real conversion, in other words, we should be looking for some real change in a person's social relations, some change in the kind of community with which the person feels at home.[2] And, behind that sequence of conversions that developmentalists term our transitions from one stage of faith to another, we should find an expansion of the range of people with whom we identify and to whom we feel responsible. The broadening vision that signals faith's maturing implies, then, a broadening of the range of people who contribute to that vision. By the same token, the limits of faith's maturity can be measured by the range of people whose experience it ignores.

The maturity of a person's faith cannot be gauged simply by the luster it sheds on the individual's life. A person's faith always says something about the group of people of which the person feels a part. There is nothing novel about this idea.[3] Faith always has to do with community. The way we see the world, including the way we think things are "in the eyes of God," inevitably has its roots in the society of which we are members. In the religious life of any social group the group itself is affirmed. The way we think about God, and what it means to be obedient to God, is shaped subtly but decisively by the needs of our social group. What it means to be holy is linked to our perception of the people of whom we are part.

What we really hold sacred—though in an unconscious, unreflective way—is our society itself, the community of those with whom our lot in life is cast. The rules that appear as inviolate are those that are linked to the cohesiveness and survival of the group. We are often dismayed by the way in which religious labels come to identify warring groups—think of Catholic versus Protestant in Northern Ireland, for example, or Christian versus Muslim in Lebanon —but we should not be surprised. Who is to be included in the community and who is to be kept out are basic societal choices. They are choices being made all the time, especially where a shift in the present boundaries is threatened. And they are choices that require religious justification.

Our Community, Our God

Even when we communicate with our God—especially when we communicate with our God—none of us

stands outside of society. The meanings that finally
ground our lives are meanings we share with others.
To be faithful is to affirm the meanings of the group
whose meanings we share. This is not to deny that we
are individuals, but it is to recognize that we are
never *merely* individuals. Nor is this something peculiar to our life in faith. Many studies have shown how
individual personality is shaped by the community of
which the individual is part. Our most basic sense of
reality, the categories in which all our thinking is
done, the range of emotional responses that stand
this side of madness, our sense of right and wrong,
beauty and ugliness, fact and illusion—every landmark by which we orient ourselves in the world, by
which we know who we are and where we stand—all
come to us as we learn the thinking, language, and
rules of our social group.[4] Just as individual identity is
rooted in social relatedness, and as faith permeates
identity, so is faith rooted in social relatedness. If our
faith names what we care about more than anything
else in life, so does it name the community we care
about more than any other.

In ancient times, people were frank about the relationship between their faith and their community. No
one pretended that God was any people's God but
theirs. The images of the tribal deities were commonly held aloft as the people did battle, founded new
settlements, and defined the rights and conditions
of citizenship. Quite unselfconsciously, religion celebrated the race, the group, the tribe. It affirmed as
sacred the blood that the people shared and the territory they staked out as their own. No question here
of who were the people of God! Our people were God's
people, our enemies God's enemies, our wars holy
wars, our armed might a divine blessing, our borders

sacred. If other peoples suffered defeat, hungered, were exiled or reduced to slavery, they had gods of their own to whom they could take their troubles.

This is not by any means to suggest that tribal society was not genuinely religious. Religion is the key to any culture. A people finds its meaning in being part of a larger context, owes its legitimacy to being part of an overall design, measures its wisdom and mores against some ultimate yardstick, explains its purposes in terms of the laws of nature, the movement of history, or the will of the gods. The social is inevitably rooted in the sacred. But, in tribal religions, the sacred essentially confirms the social, the purposes of the gods coinciding more or less neatly with the purposes of the tribe.

One Community, One God

The God of the Jews upset all this. While the priestly tradition carried on the notion that this people, our people, was God's chosen favorite, it could no longer simply be left at that. The fate of other peoples could not be relegated to other gods, for there is none other than Yahweh. Alien peoples, too, are under the care of the one and only God. This startling revelation subverts the very meaning of "enemy." It raises the deepest questions about the holiness of the nation's wars and the exclusiveness of its concerns. It challenges the nation's too easy assumption that worshipping God means looking after its own. It suggests radically new implications in the nation's covenant with God, a new sense of the responsibility of being "chosen," a new vision of the people of God. Everything is seen from a new perspective: no longer simply a national perspective, but a world perspective; no longer simply the insider's perspective, but the outsider's as well. In the worship of this God whose loving-kindness embraces every being, the measure of fidelity will always be the fate of the outsider.

In Jewish history the new vision was carried by the prophetic tradition. It would have to struggle against the constant tendency to lapse into narrow nationalism; against the tendency to settle for all the simple divisions of chosen and rejected, friend and enemy, godly and damned, insider and outsider, us and them; against every facile identification of piety and patriotism. But the prophets kept the vision alive, and the prophetic vision would again burst out with new clarity in the person of Jesus.

"Who is my neighbor?" was the question put to Jesus. Who are we commanded to love? Who are the people who matter in the eyes of God? How far do God's people extend? Who are chosen? Jesus answers with the parable of the "good Samaritan." People in need are people who matter. It is not nation, tribe, caste, or class that gives a person a claim to another's compassion; it is being beaten up and left half dead. The outcast, it seems, is more likely to understand that than even the priest or levite. Again, it is not a matter of privileged membership; it is a radically new vision of membership. It is Paul's vision of the God before whom there are no distinctions between insiders and outsiders, Jew and Greek, male and female, slave and free. It is the universalist vision that has distinguished the Yahwist tradition and shaped its concern for the world. It is a faith connected, as are all faiths, with the task of community building, but one which celebrates the whole human race as the community to be cared for. It is a faith to challenge the particular community, whatever its own interests, to

honor the interests of all. History suggests that it is
no easy faith.

The Nation's Faith

The founders of the American nation were not looking for an easy faith; it was this biblical tradition on
which they drew for inspiration. The new republic
would be no merely secular social compact, but the
bearer of eternal values; not just an agreement
among men, but a new covenant with God. For
America was the New Israel, the promised land to
which God had led his people, an Elect Nation, set
apart by Divine Providence. A single symbolic tradition linked the prophets Isaiah and Amos, Jesus and
Abraham Lincoln. Certainly, there was no conflict
here between one's civic and religious obligations:
patriotism blended with piety, civic duty with obedience to God. But the religion of the new nation should
not be dismissed as some thinly-disguised self-
worship. At its best it represented a people's attempt
to make explicit the ideals they were committed to
live by, the standards of humanity they would strive
to maintain, the yardstick against which they would
measure the quality of national life. And they were
exacting standards. If they were a chosen nation,
they were also a nation under divine judgment. The
covenant with God was both a guarantee of God's
blessing and a reminder of God's command.

Liberty and justice for all: that would be the touchstone of the political process. It would draw people
beyond their instinctual self-interest and focus their
energies on the good of all. It would guarantee protection for the poor, the powerless, the unattractive, and
the unproductive. Out of a multitude of individuals, it

would create a caring community. The nation had only one claim on the loyalty of its citizens and that was its obedience to God; and obedience to God meant fair and equal treatment for everybody. If it is difficult now to think of this national religion without a touch of embarrassment or cynicism, it should be remembered that it was once assumed by the young nation as a serious and unselfconscious commitment.

And yet is *is* hard to capture the original enthusiasm of the nation's founders. It is painful to be reminded of ideals that have become so tarnished, of glorious symbols put so often to such inglorious uses. The nation chosen by God became puffed up with self-importance, sweeping brutally over native peoples, expanding its borders by force, and imposing its will on peoples far from its shores. Its sense of being entrusted by God with a mission became its "manifest destiny," a license for a demeaning paternalism and for plunderous empire-building. The language of religion came to serve a narrow, national self-worship, an idolizing of the American Way of Life. So, with no little complacency, the United States flag in the sanctuary and patriotic hymns at Mass identify the chosen nation. The phrase "under God" is confidently added to the Pledge of Allegiance. We rest assured that God is for us and we are for God. And the chaplains bless B-52's heavy with death for our enemies. It takes years of dogged resistance on the part of a small, southeast Asian, peasant nation, a mounting clamor of world opinion, and the humiliation of defeat to bring us to our senses—and perhaps to a measure of modesty.

Veterans' Day is suddenly a sad observance, not just for the passing of comrades but for the passing of the nation's pride. They gather each year in dwindling numbers at the Eternal Light monument in Madison Square Park and in little groups across the nation. The older veterans, in their uniform caps, extol the glories of the past and berate the negativism of the new generation. The younger, Vietnam-era veterans mock the caps and carry a sign: "To hell with national pride. We'll not be used again!" The older chauvinism is sad, to be sure, but what are we to make of the new cynicism?

A sturdy national faith is a two-edged sword, at one and the same time calling the nation to responsibility and tempting it to arrogance. Think of what it means to be a "chosen" nation. How the meanings shift! Now it signifies a special moral obligation, now a cloying smugness. Now the two meanings separate, now they blend. And it is the same when the nation's faith breaks down. It cuts both ways, deflating a people's arrogance but stripping them, too, of their sense of responsibility. Perhaps, after Vietnam, we are less likely to take ourselves too seriously. We are more sensitive to the perversion of our national symbols. We have a keener ear for hypocrisy in high places. We have lost our innocence and are the wiser for it. But if we are simply disillusioned, we have also lost something of critical importance. If we have lost our arrogance, we have also lost our idealism. If our religious symbols are less likely to lull us into complacency, so are they less likely to call us to account for our conduct as a nation.

The irony of it is that the civic piety that degenerates so easily into national self-worship is the only thing capable of sustaining any serious national self-criticism. It takes a sense of being bound by covenant with God, the same sense that has hallowed the nation's worst excesses, to make us feel accountable to anything beyond our own self-interest. For all the pretensions and smugness generated by the national faith, we yet depend on it to prick our pretensions and smugness. For all the tendency to glorify the nation's narrowest self-concern, we depend on the nation's faith to challenge our narrowness and to hold up the ideal of the community in which the concerns of all are held sacred. The death of the nation's faith cuts the ground from under our pride, but also from under radical dissent, protest, and criticism. Cynicism is no challenge to conscience; only faith can provide that. If we are accountable to no higher law, then we are accountable only to ourselves.

The realization that the health of the nation depends on reverence for its symbols leads to periodic efforts to buff up the symbols, to dust off the traditional values, to call the nation back to its ideals. America's bicentennial provided us with an excuse for a flurry of activity in this regard. There was, of course, any amount of self-satisfied jingoism associated with the country's birthday celebration. But serious minds were concerned to rescue the national heritage from this kind of abuse, to restore its authority, to press it for its power to inspire us to higher things. If only we would again proclaim the ideal of liberty and justice for all, it seemed, we could not help but see how far we had fallen short of it and would emerge with new determination to put things right.

The only problem with this hope is that the loftiest civic ideals, visions, and intentions have frequently coexisted quite comfortably with the most oppressive social arrangements. In seventeenth-century America, for example, the usual way to distinguish between white and black peoples was to speak of Christians and Negroes. Being a Christian meant both a commitment to the dignity and equality of all human beings and, at the same time, the right of Christian Europeans to exclude, exploit, and enslave blacks.[5] Catholic preachers in Spain conjured up visions of universal brotherhood even as native peoples were being subjugated in Spanish America. Protestant preachers in Virginia extolled the God-given dignity of the human being even as the slaves were being unloaded in chains at the docks.

Blatant opportunism no doubt accounts for some of the discrepancy between theory and practice, and that is not difficult to understand. What is difficult to understand, however, is the easy coexistence of slavery and oppression with *sincere* professions of humanity and justice. When it comes down to what people see as the practical implications of their ideals, when it comes down to what they actually find intolerable in their society and what they actually feel moved to change, it turns out that their theoretical commitment to Christian values does not necessarily make any difference. Too often, well-intentioned commitments to universal human community prove able to settle down comfortably side-by-side with the most brutal exclusions.

To explain this fact we need return to the fundamental connection between religion and the social group: the faith that people profess always tends to strengthen the social group in which they feel at home. This means that, in our lives of faith, we are subject to a pull other than our conscious ideals and intentions. Whatever our explicit loyalties, we give implicit loyalty to the community of those with whom our lot in life is cast. Membership in that community gives us a point of view, a set of priorities, a special interest in the religious heritage, a way of interpreting it. The religious ideal may enjoy an authority more ancient than the people that professes it; the hallowed symbols may bear meanings that are not reducible to the purposes of the faithful. But how the heritage is employed concretely—its practical consequences, the purposes to which it is actually pressed—depends on the perspective of those who draw on it for the comfort, challenge, and meaning they need.

This enables us to explain, without recourse to moral cynicism or conspiracy theories, how it is that Christian nations, drawing on a religious tradition that celebrates God's concern for the whole human race, have managed to justify their imperialistic ambitions by recourse to the same tradition. What the words of the Gospel say is a matter of record. What the words are taken to mean is a matter of policy. Between the record and the policy there stands a human community, gathered in faith as a condition of survival. No doubt, the record will be sometimes distorted willfully for their convenience; but, even with good will, it will inevitably be read through their eyes, responsive to their priorities, and tailored to their needs.

Faith and the Social Structure

In thinking about the community really served by faith, it is important to note that the faith of the nation is not the faith of a homogeneous group of people. In a nation in which people have widely differing access to the common wealth, its cultural as well as its material wealth, the heritage of faith belongs more to some than to others. That is to say, some have more control of it than others, more interpretive skills and credentials, more opportunity to write and teach, more facility with the media of communication, easier access to the funding sources. These are educated people in the service of the powerful. It is not conspiracy that links them but a common perspective, the perspective of the advantaged.

The faith tradition interpreted by this professional elite lends an aura of legitimacy to the kind of society they value and of which they are themselves valued members. The social group celebrated by faith in this case is not simply an undifferentiated entity called the nation but the highly differentiated social structure in which everyone inherits, scrambles for or is assigned a place, and in which not all places are by any means equal. Faith celebrates the structure of the nation's wealth and power and signs of the celebration abound. The church's important people associate with the nation's important people. Preachers adorn presidential inaugurations and grace the East Room of the White House. A thousand sermons buttress the system with platitudes. Bishops address businessmen's luncheons. Priests bless private clubs. While, further down the scale, a "housing office" in the neighborhood rectory helps keep outsiders out. It is a religion to protect the system, a religion to sanction the borders—of nation, caste, and class.

Even in its American application, the Chosen People has never signified simply the American nation. Within this chosen people there is yet another chosen people, those favored by the social system. The architects of the nation's faith—people like Benjamin Franklin, Thomas Jefferson, and George Washington—were fired by an Enlightened concern to see religion used for worthwhile social purposes, to see it yielding the good manners, discipline, and

habits necessary to the American way of life. If religion has come to be seen as the guarantee of material
success, or the church as an instrument in bettering
one's position, and Christian ethics as the disciplined
struggle out of the slum and into a decent neighborhood, this is to be expected from the faith that affirms
the system and fosters the social mobility that the
system permits. It will, of course, have little to offer
those whom the system still depends on as a pool of
cheap and menial labor or those who simply produce
too little to fall within its ambit of concern. Pressed
into the service of the social hierarchy, even a faith
that glories in the symbols of universal human community in fact fosters the lives of a far narrower
community.

What we are speaking of here is a matter of faith's
social dynamics much more than it is a matter of its
conscious intent. In fact, the faith of those favored by
the social system not infrequently concerns itself
with the fate of those left behind by the working of the
system. The nineteenth-century anti-slavery movement is a case in point. Here is the national faith at its
best. When Abraham Lincoln lashes out against slavery in his Second Inaugural Address, he appeals to
the nation's most sacred symbols, the covenant with
God and the judgment of God, as the keys to the
nation's history. From the beginning, the abolitionist
movement drew on the religious energies of the nation. William Lloyd Garrison and Theodore Dwight
Weld stood square in the prophetic tradition. The
issue of slavery was one of sin and the Civil War a
terrible but righteous divine judgment. And the appeal to faith turned the nation around, setting the
slaves free and guaranteeing to all the equal protection of the laws. Or did it?

There seems no doubt that—whatever the economic and political causes that led to the Civil War, the emancipation of the slaves, and the Fourteenth Amendment—it was the appeal to the national faith that provided the ultimate legitimacy and sanction for these important developments. And yet the appeal to faith proved able to sanction just that degree of adjustment to the social structure that the powerful political and economic interests were ready for, and no more. Beyond that, the abolitionist movement was of profound importance to the sensitive white conscience, a drama of sin, judgment, and redemption in the white soul. White America could congratulate itself and draw satisfaction for years afterwards from the image of Lincoln freeing the slaves. Only black Americans would realize how much things had remained the same, how partial was their freedom, how much of what was gained legally was soon lost politically and socially.[6]

In the latter part of the nineteenth-century, blacks in America would be increasingly disenfranchised, segregated, terrorized, and lynched. The problem was not that the anti-slavery movement had not been a conscientious struggle—far from it—but that it had been a drama played out almost wholly in the consciences of the privileged. Even as the promises of the Reconstruction period were being abandoned and legal discrimination against blacks was sharply on the increase, conscientious whites would be shouldering the "white man's burden" in order to help the "less fortunate" in Hawaii, Cuba, and the Philippines. Appealing to the symbols of faith in order to arouse the consciences of the advantaged has always had ironic consequences for the oppressed. What is actually achieved by the way of justice—the real social result—turns out to depend less on the good will of those involved or the symbolic tradition on which they draw than on the social structure that determines their real interests, their perspective on things, and their needs. Even in the midst of its most glorious struggle for justice, the faith of the privileged turns out finally to affirm the community of the privileged.

Whether even the most uplifting symbols of justice can effectively yield any actual progress toward justice clearly depends on factors other than the abstract meaning of the symbols or the good intentions of those who would press them into the struggle. It depends on who they are who draw on the symbols for inspiration, where they find themselves in the structure of the world's power and prestige, whether they find themselves within or without the community of the advantaged and, consequently, how urgently they need things to change. In the earliest years of the nation, blacks were denied any access at all to the faith on which the nation was founded. They were chattel, and it was feared that baptism would challenge their servile status. When they *were* introduced to Christianity, it was a Christianity seen through the eyes of their masters, stressing patience, obedience, and rewards in a heaven far removed from the plantations of this world.

Blacks in Rhodesia and South Africa, and subjugated peoples in Christian empires around the world, would recognize that gospel. Its symbols were those of dignity, equality, freedom, and justice for all. They were symbols to fill white hearts with pride, to fortify white Americans in the struggle against British tyranny, even eventually to confront liberal white consciences with the evidence of their own social sins.

But they were symbols in the hands of the favored. Only in the hands of slaves and outcasts had they ever meant freedom for slaves and outcasts. Indeed, they were once the symbols of an enslaved people and they were then instruments of deliverance. Even the attenuated symbols doled out in the carefully-circumscribed catechesis of the American slaves could, in the hands of their own people, suddenly touch a nerve of the black experience, giving them words adequate to their pain and their determination to be free. In the same hands the ancient symbols can do the same today, in the hands, that is to say, of those whose Exodus to freedom still lies ahead of them. Where faith aspires to universality, its limits are no better appreciated than from the vantage point of those still excluded nor its potential better exploited than in the hands of those who depend on it for their lives.

Changing Faith, Changing Society

All this should alert us to the fact that there is always a group process underlying such phenomena as having faith, finding faith, losing faith, and growing in faith, and in the phenomenon that developmentalists describe as the transition from one faith-stage to another. There is always a community at stake, a community within the boundaries of the nation and cutting across all national boundaries. It may be a community strengthening or relaxing its borders, a community drawing tighter in defense of its own or expanding to embrace those who were once outcasts, a community entrenched or a community waiting to be born. The development of faith involves a rearrangement that is not confined to the individual psyche but touches the social order as well. It is at its core a process of ungrouping and regrouping, a withdrawal of enthusiasm from established societal rules and an investing of enthusiasm in new rules, a repudiation of the old authorities and a recognition of a new authority.

While it is psychology that has given us the developmental model, the intimate link between personal and societal life presses us to think of development in societal terms: to think of the stimulus to growth not just as the intellectual problem that challenges the settled mind, but as the outsiders threatening to penetrate the closed community; to think of the stress and adventure of stage transition not just as the substitution of new for old ideas, but as relinquishing old alliances for a new pattern of relationships; to think of wider role-taking not just as a new mental skill, but as a new community of reflection and decision-making; to think of growing universality not just as a humanitarian's expanding vision, but as the vision of an expanding human community; to think of the equilibrium we all seek by nature not just as a cohesive set of meanings in our heads, but as the just and peaceful society.

If we think of faith development as involving a remaking of society then we will not be misled into taking as real developments those "peak experiences," conversions, or other transformations of consciousness that involve no change in the social framework of our lives. The faith that does not remake society is the faith that confirms the present social arrangement. It will matter little whether faith claims to be a purely private matter between the believer and God, whether it is consciously used to firm'up the existing societal boundaries, or whether it celebrates the abstract symbols of universal community. Unless it gathers together those whom the old social structure kept apart then it is itself a buttress of the old social structure.

Faith that Builds the Human Community

A relief map of the globe, showing the highs and lows of its wealth and power, would indicate tall peaks of privilege in the developed nations, lesser peaks in the commercial centers of the developing world and, for the rest, broad and barren valleys. A world with the resources of life so concentrated and with so many people left outside the favored enclaves urgently needs the symbols of world community. But clearly, it needs more than the symbols. If we would see signs of the coming of a community in which all the world's people could feel at home, we will need to look beyond the periodic display of symbols, the periodic rhetoric of justice. We will need to look to the actual social arrangements that protect the preserves of power. We will need to look to where those left outside the gates are pressing to gain entry and where those within are reaching out to bring them in. At those points a human community is in the making.

The faith that gathers the builders together and keeps them at their task is the faith of a new community, a faith to break open the structures of exclusion, a faith to widen the group recognized as people who matter. Where faith is said to mature as it embraces the interests of a wider range of people, this dismantling and rebuilding will be the signs of its development. Where universality is faith's yardstick, one faith will be recognized as more developed than another only because it is the faith of a more inclusive community. It will be a more developed faith because it will be the faith of a community in which some participate as persons who did not previously participate. It will be a new faith, celebrating the lives of those left out of the old society and unsung by the old faith. Only as faith builds the community from which *no one* is excluded can it lay any credible claim to maturity.

The demands of a developing faith touch differently the lives of people already included in the community of those whose lives are fostered as compared to those who are not. Those favored by a social system buy into it much more deeply than is possible for those on the fringes; the included are socialized to a sense of "belonging" in a way not true of the excluded. Favored people struggling to be faithful can yet find it very difficult to withdraw their enthusiasm from the rules even of an unjust social system. Because of the profound links between personality and the society in which personality is fashioned, the fundamental changes needed to make just the unjust society will mean equally fundamental changes in the person socialized into it. Faith at this point will need to meet the challenge posed by the fact that personality is so deeply rooted in the meaning systems into which we are born, and so heavy has been our emotional investment in the existing social system, that we often feel unable to make the transition without crippling identity crises.

The quality of our faith community will be severely tested at this point. It will soon be revealed what stage of faith the community—be it the local congregation, the diocese, the religious order, or less formal group—is ready to support. If there is no community to sponsor our rising to meet the new challenges to faith, we will not likely attempt the transition. In that case, faith is simply coopted in the interests of those whose lives are fostered by the existing social arrangement. For those committed to the worship of the just God—the one and only God standing above the partisan loyalties of the tribal gods—the connection between faith and community carries both a promise and a warning. There is the promise of a faith to sustain the remaking of the world, a faith to celebrate the community in which all lives are cherished and from which no one is excluded. There is the warning that, short of the struggle to build the new community, faith may just as effectively strengthen the existing community, bolstering the privilege of the insider and shoring-up the walls against the alien.

CHAPTER 5

Faith and Authenticity

Discovering Ourselves

While the faith we profess always has to do with the social groups we belong to, faith will also have to reckon with the fact that we do not always belong quietly. Sometimes we resist belonging. Sometimes we feel smothered by belonging. At such times the group's very concern for us frustrates a new and insistent urge. It is the urge to be ourselves, to make our own choices, to take our own risks, and to shape our own destinies. At this point there is a critical shift in our feelings for the community that has accepted, defined, and nurtured us; we are no longer simply comforted but somewhat irked by its solicitude. We need to breathe the fresh, free air of independence. We need to carve out an identity we can call our own. We need to feel that we are pursuing our own aspirations and not some agenda drawn up for us and laid on us by others. It is the need for authenticity.

Ironically, not even the quest for authenticity arises as a spontaneous or individual initiative. Even at our most ruggedly independent we depend on a sponsoring community, both to whet our appetite for independence and to provide the moral support we need to pursue it. Whether we win, lose, or even join the battle for authentic selfhood will depend on what kind of company we enjoy. It will depend on what kind of support we find in the culture or at least in some countercultural movement. In some eastern cultural settings, such concern over the self might seem positively perverse. In the West, it enjoys its own cultural symbols and supports, a tradition that has waxed and waned with history. Visible as early as in the literature of the ancient Greeks and Hebrews, the problem of the authentic self was a preoccupation among the Enlightenment thinkers of eighteenth-century France and again among twentieth-century existentialists. Where the spark catches fire, it does so in the company of those who already burn for freedom. Independence is not the same as individualism, although it sometimes assumes that guise; rather, it is a matter of finding the groups we need in order to win our distance on the groups we need no longer.

For all that, it is no longer the desire to belong that marks this phase in our lives. Or at least the desire to belong is no longer a desire for security, for nurture, for the assurance that someone strong and reliable has control of our lives. Now it is a desire for self-definition and for the groups that we freely choose in the process of that self-definition.

If faith is to make adequate sense of our experience, it will have to reckon with this thirst for authenticity. The faith that usually celebrates the groups in which we feel secure will sometimes be called on to celebrate the struggle of the self against the nurturing group, the self bent on finding itself. It is a struggle waged more earnestly at some historical periods than at others and at some points in the course of individual development more than others. In fact, its emergence marks a particular milestone in the individual's life-journey and, when faith is called on at that time to make ultimate sense of what is happening, it undergoes one of those surprising transformations that we recognize as the transition from one stage of faith to another.

Though this struggle for independence does not find support in every culture, the universal history of childhood conspires to make it a necessary task of development—for we are born dependent, we learn dependence, and we are kept dependent, at least through childhood and perhaps for life. The infant's first flush of individuality—that early sense of self that comes on discovering that he or she is not the world but that the world is "out there" as a partner to be dealt with—soon fades before the evidence that it is no equal partnership. The world is already established and ordered. Reality is already defined and categorized. The rules have already been written. In the process called socialization, the individual accepts the inevitability of the social order, learns its discipline and its comforts, and takes on the identity it assigns.

Of course, the child's vision is widening, a broader range of experience being assimilated all the time. But, while reality is opening up for the individual in this way, it is not opening up at random or without pattern. Children are socialized into a particular view of the world and a particular set of values. The culture, with its prevailing myths and assumptions, becomes integrated into the individual personality. Learning the language is itself a momentous shaping process, for what the child learns is not just a vocabulary but a way of thinking and even a pattern of social relationships.[1] Words like "authority" and "obedience," "trust" and "responsibility," and the various synonyms for those who lead and those who are led, convey a whole structure of relationships and take their particular meanings from that structure. Long before we begin thinking for ourselves or making choices of our own, the context and limits of our thinking and choosing are already laid down, in the world and in our heads.

With regard to this shaping of the new generation, psychologist R. D. Laing writes: "We indicate to them how it is: they take up their positions in the space we define. They may then choose to become a fragment of that fragment of their possibilities we indicate they are."[2] We indicate to them *how it is*. What is taught is a definition of reality shaped along cultural, class, status, racial, ethnic, and sex lines. The individual is now male or female, black or white, citizen or slave, capitalist or communist, patrician or plebeian. The reality to which children are "opened up" is what is agreed upon by those social groups in which they are nurtured and with which they most closely identify.

Being born into a family is a pivotal part of the process. It is in the bosom of the family that the child learns society's definitions, rules, and requirements. Above all, it is there that the child first learns the lesson that most societies regard as crucial. For in the family the child first learns the meaning of hierarchy, that is, that some are above and some below, that some command and others obey. It would be difficult to overestimate the importance of this first and fundamental conditioning. As a way for people to relate to one another, hierarchy will seem as natural as the air we breathe. The traditional family is itself a hierarchy, and a child's experience there is an ideal preparation for taking his or her place in the hierarchy of the larger social unit, the order of the class society.[3] Few things will ever prove as difficult to question seriously as the propriety or the naturalness of a social order in which some make decisions for others.

What is not biologically given is culturally given; the point is, it is *given*. The common lot of childhood is dependency. If the struggle for authenticity—authorship of one's own ideas and choices—emerges as a universal task of development, it is because the universal experience of childhood is one of submitting to other people's ideas and choices. The development that begins in dependency can easily be arrested by that dependency. Beyond a certain point, we will not develop further unless our dependency becomes problematic. At that point, to grow will mean to take responsibility for ourselves.

Where the development of faith follows the contours of human development, it will be marked by this same passage from dependency to responsibility. If it is to develop fully, the childhood faith that is dependent on the nurturing community and derived from it will at some point have to answer for itself. The passage may not be easy, given our protracted formation in the family and in the faith that sustains it. Many adults, Laing argues, have been more or less in a hypnotic trance since early infancy. "When the dead awaken," he adds, "we shall find that we have never lived."[4] A genuinely adult faith will require at least some waking from the dead. Where faith has obediently celebrated the old order and its authorities, it will take a different kind of faith to sponsor the passage from dependency on the old to responsibility for the new. Sponsoring that passage will be the first task of adult faith.

It is not a passage that always enjoys the sponsor-

ship of the institutional church. The sturdy rebel-
liousness of most Reformers soon assumed the bur-
dens of paternal discipline. The wisdom of the an-
cients dominated the orthodox synagogue. And pre-
Vatican II Catholicism was nothing if not authoritarian. Catholics will well recall that Holy
Mother Church thought of its members as children
and fostered in them a faith that was truly childlike.
Moreover, even where institutional support for it exists, many will have little stomach for the passage and
little desire for its gains. Dependency can bring a
sense of security; frankly, it can be a comfort to have
someone else assume responsibility for one's life.
Even where people sever their ties with one nurturing community, it may simply be to find even more
security elsewhere. These are choices that, for the
moment at least, call a halt to faith's development.

Where we do embark on the passage, the authorita-
tive tradition that we have absorbed from childhood
falls into perspective. We get a view of it that we never
had before. Perhaps quite suddenly, perhaps in a slow
and barely perceptible movement, truths long taken
for granted are seen in a new, more critical light.
Authorities who have always been trusted implicitly
are held up to a new scrutiny. We discover that our
own story is only one among many, and the discovery
may well shatter our once cohesive, systematic, reliable, God-centered view of the world. Once it all hung
together; now it seems everything is open to question.
Faith has become self-conscious.[5]

A Critical Faith

This is a watershed experience for faith. We may
feel cheated or enthused. We may feel liberated or
just lost. But faith will never be the same again.

Perhaps we find that we can now believe nothing; perhaps we are able to rethink and reappropriate the tradition in a way we find satisfying. But, though the content of faith may not have changed, our way of being faithful certainly has. Though the old stories and symbols may still have meaning for us, we can now see through them; we can recognize them for what they are. Even if our questioning is rarely as profound as it feels, yet our faith *is* now a questioning faith. A new element has made its appearance in the process by which we make ultimate sense of things: the critical self has emerged as a reference point. Where we once more or less automatically interpreted our own experience of life in terms of the truths that we were taught, we now feel the need to test those truths against our own experience. Where we once felt only our obligation to the religious tradition, now we feel that the tradition owes us an obligation too. We are moving beyond dependency and naiveté; authenticity has become an element of faith.

In listening to adults trace the paths their faith has taken, one event that often stands out vividly is their breaking the boundaries of childhood faith. In some cases, breaking out may be a largely intellectual odyssey, undertaken with the aid of a few fresh books and teachers; in others, an emotionally-charged bid for personal freedom; in still others, a more protracted and demanding journey, one that is both communal and political. How dramatic a rupture is involved depends on what kind of resistance is mounted. Where people have grown up in a grandly authoritarian religious environment, like that of 1950s Catholicism, two features emerge: first, it is likely to be a hard world to break out of; but second, when you've done it, you know you've done it! By contrast, in the more permissive environment of liberal-minded families, the break tends to be both less traumatic and less clearly defined.

But the question of how thoroughgoing a rupture is involved in the passage to adult faith has to do with much more than differences in styles of piety and parenting. For running parallel with the development of childhood faith has been the child's discovery of his or her place in the social order. Just what that place is—whether the child has been nurtured within a family of the privileged, of the oppressed, or of the "kept" classes—will have an important bearing on what the maturing of childhood faith will mean. The struggle for independence, and the faith that fuels that struggle, will carry different implications for the social order in different cases, for the simple reason that the social order will permit a greater measure of freedom for some than it will for others.

Psychic Hurdles

The hierarchical society provides different opportunities of development for different people. Once authenticity and independence become issues, the child even of a class advantaged by society faces a tough developmental hurdle, but one which is likely to be more psychological than societal. Relationships with parents and with the other authorities who have both blessed and dominated childhood will need to be renegotiated. Moreover, we will need to come to grips with the child within as well as with the authorities without. An adolescent rebellion may begin the process and any number of stormy separations may appear to resolve it; but it is a lengthy, perhaps a lifelong, task. Periodically we will feel satisfied that

we have discovered our true self, until some still truer
self demands recognition. Early selves may emerge
bristling with defenses, all temper, vanity, and im-
petuosity. We will expect the later self to be more
confident in its choices, steadier in its convictions,
surer of itself.

The search for the self that begins as a preoccupation with cutting ties, defining boundaries, and ac-
centuating the new image with bold strokes can be
expected to mellow, to be more compassionate and
understanding of others, to settle eventually into the
tranquility of a more seasoned wisdom. The discovery of this strong and gentle self will be no mean
achievement. Even where society throws up no special obstacles of poverty, prejudice, or powerlessness,
our timid psyches will offer resistance enough. It will
take a sturdy faith to press us continually beyond the
petty and familiar. True magnanimity is a hard-won
beauty. At this stage of faith, for those of us unen-
cumbered with more political objectives, it is what
saving our souls is all about.

Political rhetoric can sometimes disguise for a time
what is an essentially personal quest for authenticity.
Many of the campus radicals of the late sixties, for
example, found companionship and encouragement
in militantly countercultural groupings and explained their struggle in the language of radical social
change. While their claims to a new, critical awareness were often genuine enough, they were generally
well-advantaged by the existing social arrangement
and time would tell that they had no long-standing
differences with it. The rhetoric of social criticism
clothed a struggle for authentic selfhood that was not
essentially social but personal, familial, and generational. Indeed, even as a quest for personal indepen-

dence, it was frequently satisfied with remarkably modest gains: the angry young radical quickly settled into middle-class complacency.[6] But, even where its sights are set high, there is no compelling reason why the concern of the advantaged for their self-development should affect a society that in large measure values and fosters it.

Being oneself, taking responsibility for one's own life and choices, is a very different proposition for those who are disadvantaged by the arrangement of society. It is one thing to take one's place as a critical and accomplished adult in a society where that is recognized as one's prerogative, quite another where it is seen as an effrontery or a threat. And the fact is that the hierarchical society into which all are socialized intends different prerogatives for its different members. Nor is there anything haphazard about the arrangement. The rules that guarantee opportunities for development to some and deny them to others may be largely unspoken, but they will be clear enough in their actual working. They will take into account wealth, breeding, race, nationality, and sex. They will admit a few to the echelons of power. They will ensure that some others are at least well-kept —given some space for growth and at least a measure of control over their lives. And they will systematically lock some in dependency. To the extent that the rules frustrate them, there is no way that people can develop without changing the rules. In their case, development is a political task.

Social Hurdles

There is a sense in which the first dawning of adult faith is the same for everyone who experiences it. In all cases the experience enjoys the same abstract features—independence, initiative, responsibility —that have been gathered here under the term "authenticity." But, in the concrete, the implications of this transition will differ widely, not least its implications for the social order. In all cases, the rhythm of stress and stability that marks the process of development involves not just the fragmentation and restoration of individual meanings but some unmaking and remaking of social bonds. We grow by entering on new times and new company. For some, development will be possible by a relocation *within* the existing social order; for others, for whom the existing order provides little or no space for development, it will be possible only in the company of those bent on building a social order in which they *can* gather for development.

If our experience has been that of the dominant—or at least well-kept—social classes, our development will never have entailed anything like a fundamental social upheaval. The implications for society of a person's development—how radical an unmaking and remaking of social bonds is required—depends on that person's place in society. To the extent that we feel at home in the existing social structure, it is that structure that our faith will affirm. To the extent that people feel alien within it, they will not be able to share the faith that affirms it. In this case, if they are to share a faith that is responsive to their own needs for development, it will be with those who gather to undo the old structure and build the new. The faith that fosters the development of those within the social system and favored by it is not yet the faith that would foster the development of those excluded by the system. That will be the faith of those struggling to construct a new system.

In his biography of Paul Tillich, Rollo May refers to the common compulsion of the young to "throw a bomb" into their parents' faith "which in many cases was no great faith anyway, but chiefly a deep sense of the importance of not smoking, swearing or drinking alcohol."[7] In this situation, of course, smoking, swearing, and drinking alcohol are flaunted as the very banners of independence. They become the issues around which the generations polarize, tension is heightened, boundaries are drawn, and sides taken. And if the old faith will not bless the bid for freedom, a new faith certainly will. For every passage, there is a rite. Whatever the personal significance of this passage, however, it is of little political significance. A renegotiation between generations, it is no threat to the political and economic status quo but a part of it. And the rite that legitimates the passage is part of the faith that legitimates the system as a whole.

But think of the same passage on the part of those whom the system does not welcome as independent, adult participants: the poor, the chronically jobless, blacks, the colonized, the masses in economically dependent nations. Think of a young Malcolm X, struggling to assert his black manhood in a society that has no place for the likes of him. What is involved here is no mere transfer of power between generations. As a boy, he had often heard his father close the meetings of Marcus Garvey's Universal Negro Improvement Association with a rousing "Up, you mighty race, you can accomplish what you will!" He had seen the system squeeze the sanity out of his "welfare mother." Generational issues had long been overshadowed by political issues. Independence could never simply mean quitting the parental hearth. It had to mean assaulting the system that oppressed his people. And it found sponsorship in the brotherhood of Black Muslims. For this passage, too, would need a rite to bless it.[8]

Especially where authenticity requires the entrance of a people into a community in which they are presently denied full participation and their equal access to life-possibilities presently unavailable to them, achieving it will depend less on a rugged individualism than on fashioning a strong group identity. In a sense it remains even in this case the classic quest for a meaning which is truly one's own, but the meaning which is one's own is worked out in the common quest for the meaning which is that of one's people. Sometimes, as Harvey Cox has observed, it finds expression in the people's traditional religion,

> its testimony, . . . its stated claim to identity and dignity, . . . a way of crying, remembering, aspiring, . . . an embattled folk's only way of fighting back, . . . one way it saves its soul.

But often it has to be rediscovered. The spirit of a people has been seduced

> when these authentic inner impulses are twisted into instruments of domination. People's needs and hopes are cleverly parlayed into debilitating dependencies. The timeless stories they lived by are incorporated into a set of meanings supplied by the conqueror.[9]

Authenticity then requires that a people win back the meanings coopted by the conqueror.

Exiled Brazilian educator Paulo Freire has described the special problem that achieving authentic existence presents for the oppressed. They suffer, he says, from a deep division within themselves. "Although they desire authentic existence, they fear it. They are at one and the same time themselves and the oppressor whose consciousness they have internalized." Their conflict lies in facing the choice between ejecting the oppressor within and not ejecting him, between following prescriptions and having choices, between being spectators and being actors, between accepting and changing the conditions of their lives. It is a conflict that their education must take into consideration. To "banking" education—the "depositing" in oppressed peoples of a worldview construed from the standpoint of the advantaged—Freire contrasts "conscientization"—the emergence in the oppressed of their own authentic point of view, a critical consciousness resulting from "their intervention in the world as transformers of that world."[10] Authenticity is to be won in changing the political structures that deny it and in solidarity with one's class.

Implications for Ministry

Freire's description of the conflict in the hearts of the oppressed contains a serious lesson for any who, coming from the position and perspective of the advantaged, would instruct the poor, minister to them, or who are otherwise committed to their development. If we generalize from our own experience of development, which may entail little if any need to transform political structures, we misunderstand the implications of development for the oppressed. Our ministry will then unconsciously coopt their struggle for freedom; it will become instead yet another instrument of domination. The deep distrust evident among powerless peoples of even the best-intentioned ministrations of the powerful should be seen against this background. As long as a people's prospects for development rest on their struggle for social change, our ministries will need to celebrate that struggle if they are to be helpful for development. In fact, they will need to do so if they are to be ministries of faith at all and not merely tools of pacification. Growing in faith is, for the oppressed, a political act.

Some image of mature faithfulness inevitably informs our preaching and teaching in the local church. One catechism currently in use at least has the virtue of fleshing out quite concretely the image of holiness that inspires it. This is done in a concluding section made up of some thumbnail sketches of ordinary faithful people. They include models for the poor and models for the rich. The model for the rich we will return to later. For the poor, there is a picture of a Chicano—in overalls, smiling broadly, and standing before a U.S. flag. The accompanying text reads:

Ignacio, a migrant worker, spends long hours in the field, harvesting whatever crop he is hired for. His family lives in a ramshackle hut on the edge of town, and what they have for furniture would be thrown out by most families. "Maria is a good woman," Ignacio says. "She minds the kids and puts up with me. I wish I could give her nice clothes to go to church in."[11]

The desirable virtues are all spelled out: patriotism, hard work, thrift, gratitude, resignation, marital fidelity, a distant reverence for the consumer society and loyalty to the church. No mention is made of the courage, perseverance, critical spirit, hope, or collective solidarity of the migrant farm workers' struggle for justice. There is no Exodus image here that might stir a communal hope, inspire a political act, or disturb the security of a contented serfdom. There is no hope here of sponsoring the passage to adult faithfulness. This is not education in faith; it is pacification.

It has been said that the contemporary religious scene in the U.S. is characterized by "an intense preoccupation with authentic personal experience."[12] What needs to be kept in mind is that authentic personal experience is much more accessible to some than it is to others. The authenticity available to the disadvantaged only in a transformed society may well be available to the advantaged in a transformed consciousness. For this reason, especially if our attention is focused on the development of the advantaged, we can easily lose sight of the political and social dimensions of authentic experience and the faith that celebrates it. Evidence of this myopia may be found in the experimentation in recent years with a wide variety of supposedly "private" religious experiences—including at least some of the present preoccupation with the mystical traditions of the East and West, with "altered states of consciousness," parapsychological phenomena, the "human potential" movement, encounter and sensitivity groups, charismatic prayer groups, and the seemingly endless varieties of faddish navel-gazing.

Some have interpreted this development as a fruit of the secularization of modern society. Religion is supposed to have retreated from the social sphere to the purely personal and interpersonal spheres.[13] The interpretation is misleading. It should not be thought that religion has severed its ties with the social structure. The religion that fails to call society to account is the religion that at least implicitly maintains society. In the class society, the faith that fosters the personal development of the advantaged classes need not call society into question. But that is not a faith without ties to the class society; it *is* the faith of the class society.

To the extent that the unjust society provides a comfortable place for us we need not pay any special attention to it; it is not a problem for us. But it is a severe threat to the maturing of our faith. The danger is that, once we have won our own personal battle for recognition in the system, our faith will take on the character of an in-group celebrating its own solidarity against the intrusion of those still outside and clamoring for recognition. No faith still focused on the development of its own group is yet the faith that adequately celebrates a human community in which *all* are welcomed. History gives us too many examples of newly-enfranchised groups, their own struggles behind them, hardening in resistance against those still disenfranchised. And yet, even at this stage of faith's development, the oppressed bear in a special way the promise of a human community and a faith to celebrate it, if only for the reason that their needs for development, unlike ours, cannot be dissociated from the need to dismantle the walls of the exclusive society.

CHAPTER 6

Faith and Justice

The Progressive Parish

The *National Catholic Reporter* recently invited responses to a reader's request for help in locating a parish with an "up-to-date" outlook. What was wanted, it was explained, was a "creative, caring parish"—as distinct from the traditional "pay, pray, and obey" variety. The response was enthusiastic. "Happiness is our parish," exclaimed one editorial. Readers told of parishes that were friendly, cooperative, and small enough to permit a sense of face-to-face companionship. These were parishes blessed by intelligent and liberal-minded pastors, who encouraged wide participation in parish activities and sometimes in making parish decisions. They offered mini-courses on subjects of interest to parishioners. They were engaged in a variety of services to the poor, the elderly, and the sick. They were ecumenical, involved in the wider community, and not forgetful of social issues either. They appeared to be places where some imagination went into preparing the liturgies, where the priests were casual about status, the sermons unlikely to be condescending, the talents of parishioners appreciated, the kiss of peace heartfelt, where people stopped and talked to one another after Mass, where the faith felt alive, and Christian responsibilities extended beyond Sunday morning.[1]

Clearly, these parishes are seen as bright spots on an otherwise dull horizon. They are communities of faith where many thinking, liberal, adult Catholics are able to feel at home. As far as the development of faith is concerned, they appear as havens for many "authentic" Catholics seeking refuge from the childlike Catholicism still widely institutionalized in the traditional parish. As such they represent a real gain for faith, a decisive step beyond our earlier naiveté and dependence. We need them.

To experience our own "growing up" in faith is to seek the company of those who have similarly come of age. While the *NCR* correspondence suggests that adult company is by no means the rule in the local parishes, it nevertheless can be found and is obviously rewarding for those who find it. There is all the satisfaction of finding oneself on a new plateau in the upward journey of faith. A sense of things fitting together again, a meshing of one's diverse truths and loyalties, a resolution of conflict. Here the old truths take on fresh meaning, symbols long beaten down into one dimension swell with new life, a routinized liturgy recaptures its power to move and inspire. In fact, once one has found one's "creative, caring" parish, it is tempting to think that one has arrived.

Beyond Authenticity

This is partly, but only partly, true. An important crossing has been negotiated; another lies ahead. For, while authenticity is the first task of adult faith, it is not its only task. If adult faith faces its first challenge when it has to take responsibility for the critical self, it faces yet another when it is called to take responsibility for the world. As heavy as is faith's responsibility for the critical self, this remains a responsibility to *the self*. As important as it is to discover the faith that is true to one's own best insights, and the community which will nurture it, the faithful community is at this stage still preoccupied with *its own*. Moving beyond this stage will mean breaking out of this identification with our selves and the community in which our selves have been nurtured. It will mean reconciling our own authenticity with the authenticity of other peoples. The focal point of faith will be then no longer just the authentic self finding freedom in community with its own, but a world of authentic selves finding freedom in a community of communities. A universalist faith matures only as the faithful come credibly to identify with the peoples of the whole world.

We do not begin to make this crossing until we have been jolted out of the group consciousness which is native to us or to which we have become conditioned. We do not begin to make it without coming to know something of the limits of even our best insights, the partiality of our loyalties, the exclusiveness of our commitments, the parochialism of our community. Like every movement from one stage of development to another, it involves a profound change in consciousness. And, like every profound change in consciousness, it involves a realignment of our social ties. If faith comes to include a vantage-point from which the interests and inherited biases of our own group are truly opened to a fresh view and subject to a new criticism, this will be a sign that the faith community has broadened to include those of different interests and perspectives than our own: a new faith because new company.

The faith of this broader community will be hardly

content to celebrate *our* adult participation in communal life but will celebrate the participation of the newcomers as well. That is always the sign of growing faith. The faith that is satisfied with the welfare of its own is faith at a standstill. The mark of a developing faith is its embrace of the outsider. And, where universality is the measure of its maturity, maturing faith will be recognized by its concern for the outsider *as such*, its persistent outreach to those still excluded.

Justice Is Essential

To speak of a faith focused on the inclusion of the outsider as an adult participant in communal life is to speak of a faith for which social justice is an *essential* concern. By this definition, mature faith is of its very nature a faith to celebrate the remaking of the world in justice.

In making this claim, however, it is important to recall that the model of development to which we are appealing here measures faith's maturity not by its content but by its dynamics. It is not the *what* of faith that matters but the *why*. The fact that a faith is caught up with "justice" issues does not of itself tell us anything about faith's maturity. For faith may focus on these issues for a variety of reasons. An essentially conformist faith may involve itself in justice concerns simply out of obedience to traditional authorities. Catholics schooled in the social encyclicals of Leo XIII and Pius XI, for example, may have been committed to the labor movement for the same reason they went to Sunday Mass—namely, that both carried the blessing and weight of church authority. Alternatively, social concerns may provide the vehicle for a young person's working out what are essentially personal issues—generational conflict or an identity crisis. And the struggle for justice will inevitably characterize the efforts of oppressed peoples to win for themselves an authentic self-definition. The point is, the immediate concern for justice may spring from a variety of more fundamental objectives. And, where it is a question of reckoning faith's level of development, it is not the immediate concern but the underlying social dynamic that counts.

While not every concern for social justice arises from mature faith, every mature faith implies a concern for social justice. Action for justice is the defining feature of mature faith. There is nothing arbitrary about this designation. It flows from the recognition that faith is as mature as participation in the faithful community is broad. Faith develops along with the community whose life it celebrates: the more inclusive the community, the more developed the faith. In this view of faith's growth, the most mature faith is that which celebrates the life of the universal human community, the faith of the society in which full participation is open to all. Only where such a fellowship is being pieced together does faith begin to mature. Nor can there be any question as to what its basic agenda will be: dismantling those social institutions that divide and exclude people and replacing them with those that enable everyone to participate in communal life as valued members. If the mark of our maturity as believers is the action we take to transform the world in justice, it is simply because that is what it takes to broaden the community of those whose lives are valued. Opening up the company of the included to embrace those formerly excluded *is* the effective pursuit of justice.

Short of remaking the world in justice, faith may

yet be busy with many creative tasks, but this essential task will remain undone. Short of this transition, faith must spend itself on what are essentially our own concerns. To say that mature faith is distinguished by the fact that the works of justice make up its basic agenda is by no means to suggest that mature believers will be any the less concerned with the cultivation of the interior life, with individual healing or with works of mercy. But it is to suggest that, in the midst of all these pursuits, they will be responsive to the claims of justice—the questions, namely, of whose interests are finally served by their piety, how it affects the world's structures of wealth and power, and what bearing it has on the lives of people excluded or belittled by those structures.

Faith and Politics

A faith so committed to remaking the divided world is clearly a political faith. And faith's political implications have always proven troublesome to some. Fulminations about "keeping the church out of politics," however, can obscure the fact that the church is *always* in politics. The activity of the church in defining and celebrating the faith is always tied to a political structure, a polis, a people. It is never a question of *whether* the church will be political but only of *what kind* of political structure it will bless and celebrate. That will depend on who the faithful people are and on their faith's level of development.

At each stage of development, faith will include some conception of the right, godly, and natural way for people to relate to one another. A dependent faith might well be happy with the notion of hierarchy, reconciled to a social structure in which some command and others obey. The faith of people bent on their own authenticity will at least reject the notion of dependence *for themselves*. A faith concerned with the authentic participation *of all* will necessarily reject the very notion of social hierarchy, working to replace the structures of domination and dependence with structures that enable all to share as adults in making the decisions that matter to them. If faith develops as the community of faith grows more inclusive, we can expect that as faith develops its political implications will become increasingly democratic and participatory.

None of this is to suggest that mature faithfulness commits one to a single, specific political program. The symbols of a universalist faith are inevitably distorted when they are pressed to support a particular reading of the political signs of the times or a concrete remedy for social injustice. The political implications of a faith that would celebrate the adult participation of all cannot be appreciated from any one standpoint or spelled out in the program of any doctrinaire elite, whether or not it dons the mantle of justice. When this is forgotten, faith easily legitimates new forms of violence, new tactics of repression, and brutal new distinctions between the godly and the damned. Warriors armed with faith are notoriously more destructive than those armed with sten guns alone. A truly universalist faith will maintain its critical distance on any particular prescriptions for the common weal. In this regard, the biblical tradition bids us be mindful of the final judgment before which all this world's regimes and revolutions lie open to scrutiny and correction.

Is there, then, no connection between the New Jerusalem and all our worldly Jerusalems? Are there

no reliable distinctions to be drawn between the faithful and the faithless political response in our times?
May we faithfully evade this world's political tasks by
taking refuge in some other world or in the realm of
abstract ethical principles? Does the Gospel provide
us with no ethical guides to action? One thing is certain: to take such "apolitical" positions is not to remain politically neutral; it is simply to trim our faith
to the prevailing political givens.

For Christians, Jesus is the norm. If he rejected the
political program of the Zealots, it was hardly because
his life or message lacked political implications. For
how then would we explain the threat he represented
to the political powers of his day? Jesus died precisely
because his identification with the powerless was rife
with political implications. The judgment of universalist faith falls not on political activity as such but on
the politics of exclusion. It is not the effort to fashion
political structures that faith condemns, but the efforts that leave some human beings out of the reckoning.

Between Principle and Program

Universalist faith is not defined by the political
struggle; it defines the struggle. And yet it defines it
in recognizable ways. If it does not specify tactics,
neither does it leave us in the sphere of broad ethical
abstractions. If it does not bless a particular political
strategy, neither does it permit us to settle for a general political scepticism. While it allows for a plurality
of political interpretations and choices, it does not
follow that any interpretation or choice is as faithful
as any other. For, while faith does not hold up a concrete political program, it does hold up a model of

human relationship. It is that model of human relationship that provides the church with a link between broad moral imperative and concrete political program, enabling it to give some specificity to the one even while maintaining some critical distance on the other.

Mature faith is the faith of the inclusive human community—if not yet realized, at least in the making. It celebrates the society in which the perspectives of all groups are encompassed, their welfare pursued, and their authenticity fostered. The broad structural features of such a society seem obvious enough. The generation of wealth and the ordering of priorities will be consciously directed toward the fulfillment of human needs. Resources will be allocated according to a calculus of public rather than private welfare. The large-scale means of production and social planning in areas of such decisive importance as housing, health care, education, and transportation will be subject to effective democratic control rather than the prerogative of private groups deciding on the basis of their own commercial interests. The faith that celebrates the vocation of all as responsible human beings implies a social structure in which people are enabled to govern themselves.

Taking Sides

What bothers some people about a "political" faith—more correctly, one that is explicit about its political allegiances—is the idea that it commits a supposedly universal church to "taking sides." Several points need to be made here by way of response. First, there *is* undoubtedly such a phenomenon as a one-sided faith—commonly, that of advantaged

groups bent on protecting their own privileged position—and it has nothing to do with the development of a universalist faith. Though it may coopt the
symbols of the universalist tradition, it distorts those
symbols. In truth, it represents a failure of faith; in
biblical terms, it is idolatrous faith.

Not every partisan commitment, however, is of this
kind. An appreciation of the stages of faith's development can be helpful here. Understanding the
end-point of the process of development enables one
to locate and criticize the various stages of the
process—that is, to put an immature faith "in its
place"—but it also helps one respect the integrity of
the preliminary stages. Concern for the end of the
process implies concern for the process itself, and a
concern for the process implies a respect for the integrity of each stage and the necessary sequence of
stages.

Growing toward a mature faith, understood as the
faith of a community open to all as adult participants,
demands that all those groups historically locked into
positions of dependence be permitted to come of age.
Their coming of age may well require of them an over-
riding concern for their own identity, cohesiveness
and empowerment; a defining of boundaries; a special
emphasis on the sisterhood, brotherhood, comrade-
ship, or solidarity of the group.

In this regard, black, feminist, and Third World
theologies are frequently explicit about the partisan
character of their faith. While the partisan faith of
groups still preoccupied with their struggle for empowerment may fall short of a universalist faith,
however, it is not incompatible with it. The faith of
oppressed groups, binding them in solidarity and
blessing their efforts to throw off the yoke of the op-

pressor, is integral to their development and to the eventual construction of a universal community of peers. Not yet fully mature, it is at least on the way to maturity. And it is an indispensable stage on the way to maturity. For, without their own empowerment, oppressed peoples could enter any wider community only as dependents. That is the arrangement they have traditionally been offered; it has nothing to do with the universal community celebrated by mature faith. That kind of community can grow out of the dialogue that is possible only when oppressed groups have successfully struggled for their own truth and the right to speak it.[2]

We will expect that the mature faith that celebrates the building of the inclusive human community will be careful not to isolate or deny the humanity even of the oppressor. It will press the struggle for justice in such a way as to offer redemption to the sinner as well as to those sinned against. And yet it will press the struggle none the less vigorously for that; and the struggle will inevitably require partisan commitments. For, as long as some groups struggle to maintain the world's entrenched privilege and systematic exclusions, those who would build the inclusive society must struggle against them. As long as social structures do in fact set people against one another as haves and have-nots, building the just society demands that the faithful take sides with the have-nots.

The biblical story gives us no reason to expect that it would be otherwise. In the scriptural account of the deliverance of the oppressed Israelites, God took sides. In a racist society, as theologian James Cone points out, God is never color-blind:

In the New Testament, Jesus is not *for all*, but for the oppressed . . . and against the oppressors. The God of the

biblical tradition is not uninvolved or neutral regarding
human affairs. . . . He is active in human history, taking
sides with the oppressed of the land.[3]

Loving Everybody

In this context, theologians of liberation raise the
serious question as to what extent the church can
with integrity affirm Christian unity, or celebrate the
Eucharist as a sign of that unity, when in fact the
church indiscriminately embraces both oppressor
and oppressed.[4] For their part, critics of liberation
theology see in this unabashedly partisan stance the
denial of something sacred, a failure to affirm what
theology must affirm at all costs: the unity of all people in view of their common humanity and vocation.
The line separating oppressor and oppressed, it is
argued, is not a line that runs *between* people but
through us all. Where people *are* divided from one
another, the Gospel calls us beyond dividedness to
reconciliation and community. It is a matter of absolute importance, they argue, that the Eucharist not
become an instrument of partisan political causes and
that even if there be no other place—especially if
there be no other place—the Eucharist remain an
event around which people on both sides of the barricades can gather. To lose that vantage-point, so the
argument runs, is to make the barricades sacred—
and that is how war becomes holy.[5]

At one point in a United Farm Workers' film a priest
celebrates the Eucharist on an altar draped with a
farm worker flag, in a vestment adorned with the
Aztec eagle in place of the cross. To wince at that
scene is to feel for the critics' argument. For all that

the argument is spurious. For, in the face of actual structures of exclusion, it falsely opposes, on the one hand, the struggles of the oppressed for inclusion and, on the other, the affirmation of an inclusive human community. Not only are these things not in opposition to each other, but it is the very affirmation of inclusive community that makes holy the struggles of the excluded for inclusion. In a situation of structured social division, it is universal love that demands a commitment to the class struggle.[6]

Universalist rhetoric can easily be made to serve the interests of those in power. This happens whenever "our common humanity" is stressed in such a way as to divert attention from the social structures that actually divide people from one another. It happens whenever the need for reconciliation is stressed in such a way as to undercut the struggles of oppressed peoples for justice. It happens whenever the personal and conciliatory aspects of the Gospel are emphasized to the exclusion of its political and conflictual aspects.[7] We should not be deceived. Despite its celebration of the whole human community, this is a decidedly exclusivist faith, its grand theological abstractions quite unrelated to the concrete freedom of dependent peoples. While a world structured in oppression needs a faith that would take us *through* the revolution, such a faith would simply lead us *around* it.[8]

Getting over Anguish

Alternatively, the complexity of social issues can provide us with a convenient smokescreen in which to lose ourselves. Every problem turns out to be multifaceted; serious issues generate persuasive arguments for and against; actors on every side betray a mixture of motives. The challenge of faith is to be aware of the complexities without being blinded by them, to acknowledge the ambiguity and yet to act. While faith cannot be reduced to political analysis and strategy, it remains ineffective without them. Recognizing the inevitability of sin in human society, we must yet reject sinful structures. Acknowledging the impossibility of a perfect human society, we must yet build a better one than the one we have. Conscious of the corruption of power, we must yet immerse ourselves in the realities of power.[9]

There is nothing wrong with a lively sense of the ambiguities of human action; indeed, we would be foolish to lose it. But we need to cultivate at least as lively a sense of the way we *use* ambiguity to justify inaction when inaction best serves our own interests. Failing action, we settle for anguish. Ambiguity becomes then something more than a philosophical insight; for those advantaged by the status quo, it is a political strategy. On the other hand, when the victims as well as the beneficiaries of the unjust society are included in the process of reflection, moral issues have a way of assuming a new simplicity. Again, the lesson is clear: whether issues of injustice move the faithful community beyond anguish to action will depend on whose interests the community encompasses. It is because mature faith encompasses the victims of oppression that it is marked by action to change the oppressive society.

Worshipping the One and Only God

In a world dotted with islands of the privileged amid a vast sea of refugees and outcasts, there are as many faiths as there are peoples: faiths to fortify the strong and to pacify the weak; faiths to justify, for insiders and outsiders alike, the barriers that keep them apart. This is the faith of tribes, still tied to the worship of tribal gods. Its works are the survival and defense of the tribe. It is a faith that serves the stronger tribes well. It is a faith that many of us are content to live by, even if it contradicts the faith that we profess. Clearly, it will take a different kind of faith to celebrate the universal community, a faith open to the worship of the one-and-only God, its agenda the works of justice.

Somebody once remarked that the Eucharist that does not provoke a crisis is celebrated in heresy. It is a truth easily lost amid the rhetoric of reconciliation that proliferates whenever the nation grows weary of conflict. The divisiveness of the civil rights movement and of the Vietnam years is lamented and best forgotten; a new calm is welcomed on the campuses; spirituality turns its focus again on inner experience; prayer groups blossom in the parishes. The last thing anyone wants is another crisis, least of all in the liturgy. And, where faith is preoccupied with other tasks, divisive issues need not disturb the harmony of the eucharistic community. So, in the brutal society, the Mass celebrates the quiet violence of order. Is heresy too strong a word for this faithlessness?

Wherever faith is bent on building the truly reconciled (as distinct from the merely pacified) society, the Eucharist will be divisive, exposing the discrepancies between the Gospel we profess and the oppression we tolerate, and pressing us to align ourselves either with those who would change the system or those who would resist the change. For Christians, whether or not our local churches are able or willing to sponsor their members in moving beyond the defense of the tribe to the building of the just society will be the measure of whether the Gospel image of the kingdom of God is coming to realization in our lives.

CHAPTER 7

Faith and Affluence

A Portrait of the Rich and Decent Man

The first Christians were mostly poor. The faith that took root among them was a poor people's faith, shaped by the experience of poor people, responsive to the hopes of poor people. The "good news" was that the poor, of all people, were favored by God. People of no account by the world's reckoning, they were in a special way bearers of the Spirit of God. Powerless, they were heirs to God's kingdom. Wealth and power were, in the light of this new-found faith, not assets but liabilities.

As the Christian community came to include more people of affluence and importance, however, it gradually retreated from this original position. While poverty might still be embraced—as a "counsel of perfection"—by a religious elite, it was no longer of special significance to ordinary Christians. Nor was wealth seen any longer as a particular liability: for those favored by God were by now not the poor but rather those who gave of their wealth to the poor. As it came to reflect the experience and aspirations of a different class of people, the notion of Christian holiness had taken on a different meaning.

This revised version of holiness has generally been congenial to those of us who would be faithful to the Gospel and yet find ourselves among the world's affluent third, for it suggests that Gospel faithfulness is in some way compatible with our continuing upward mobility, our various struggles for money, security, connections, beauty, success, and power. The same catechism cited earlier for its portrait of the docile farm worker as a model for the poor gives us an equally remarkable model for the affluent. Our contemporary saint is in this case a successful banker. Affluent, he rightly enjoys the rewards of his achievements. Frankly capitalist, he is nevertheless a kind-hearted capitalist. He is powerful but without arrogance. He is businesslike, but a family man too. Quite uncritical of the socio-economic system, he is yet capable of personal warmth and compassion for the poor. He is cool under fire. He responds to conflict with civility. He is, in short, both a rich and decent man. And, in a world increasingly angry over injustice, he provides a model for the Christian who would better cope with his own guilt and other people's hostility without unduly disturbing his security or the system that guarantees it.[1]

Is this the image that we would celebrate in the local church as a model of contemporary holiness? Do we have here a catechesis in any way adequate for preparing First World Christians to respond faithfully to the demands of the Third World for justice? Where mature faith celebrates the community of those who labor to build the new world society, what would the maturing of faith mean for those favored by and socialized into the old society? Other images come to mind, no easy images of urbane benevolence, but disturbing images, Gospel images: a rich young man turning away sadly; a camel eye-to-eye with a needle.

Wealth and the Gospel

The Gospel that was originally hailed as good news for the poor is still news for the non-poor as well, though it is not the news that the non-poor frequently read it for. The wealthy and powerful have long taken hold of the Gospel as of everything else, wresting from it a comfort that was intended for the poor. But the Gospel that confirms the poor is the Gospel that rebukes the rich. What is for the Third World a promise of deliverance is for the First World a summons to repentance. As First World Christians we cannot ignore that summons without abusing the Gospel. And abuse it we do whenever we invoke it to justify our lives, as if it had nothing to say about our privilege, our conspicuous consumption or our distance from the poor.

If the Gospel recognizes the possibility of a good rich person, Gérard Lutte points out, it is "the one who does what Zaccheus did, one who is converted to justice and therefore renounces being rich."[2] As theologies of liberation emerge to articulate the hopes of the world's poor, Marie Augusta Neal has suggested, affluent peoples need to work out a parallel theology of relinquishment—a theology of letting go—to guide them to a faithful response.[3] The only faithful response, according to Gutiérrez, is "solidarity with the poor, . . . which must manifest itself in specific action, a style of life, a break with one's social class."[4] The problem with our portrait of the rich and decent man is that our wealth is itself indecent.

In the light of the Gospel, the problem with the gross maldistribution of the world's wealth has to do with the kind of relationship among people that this imbalance both reflects and perpetuates. It has to do with the assumptions it reveals about who matters and who does not. By contrast to the religion of ancient Egypt, where it was made clear that even in the next life kings were still destined to rule and serfs to serve, the blessed community envisioned by the Gospel is a community of equals. The Gospel categories of rich and poor, accordingly, refer not only to the possession of material goods but to the kind of relationships people have with one another. Wealth refers not only to material abundance but to power, prestige and position—and to the opportunities for domination and manipulation that these things afford. Conversely, the renunciation of wealth is valued as a condition of surrendering the opportunity to dominate others and accepting equality with them.[5]

Wealth and the Maturing of Faith

This Gospel image of the blessed community corresponds with the image of mature faithfulness gleaned in our review of the dynamics of faith development. The conversion that the Gospel requires of the non-poor corresponds to what we have previously described as their transition to a fully mature stage of faith. As the celebration of the inclusive community-in-the-making, mature faith challenges the affluent to relinquish their advantage. It is no arbitrary challenge. Repudiating the hierarchy of privilege is simply *what it means* to build the inclusive community; entering a community of equals is what it means to recognize all as valued participants in communal life.

If the current research into faith development is to be coopted to the service of the established social hierarchy, it will be done by denying the necessity of this relinquishment or by minimizing its implications. It will be done, for example, by defining mature faith in terms of a keener sensitivity to injustice but not in terms of taking action to change things, or in terms of some broadened "community of identification" that doesn't demand of the comfortable any real change in the circumstances of our lives. This is consciousness-raising without vulnerability. Away from the action, at sufficient emotional and geographical distance that the suffering of the poor is not seen or heard clearly enough to have any real claim on the believer, consciousness-raising is simply rationalization, a way to keep our heads together even as the world's evils press on around us.[6]

We can easily maintain our liberal, even radical, credentials without getting involved. We will give what we can afford to the right causes, sign the right advertisements and manifestos, pay our dues to the right organizations. We will learn to produce a nicely crafted statement on the current controversies, a balance of righteousness and indignation. We can expect to be reinforced by the anger of our enemies and the admiration of our friends. The stands we take may be hailed as courageous, our voices as prophetic. Our faith will have given us an image, a position on the issues, a definition of ourselves. It need not have cost us anything nor changed our lives. Nor will it have undergone any real maturing. That will entail, for the affluent, some real relinquishment, some important existential choices: about where and how we will live, about the work we will do, about the risks we will assume—and, especially, about the company we will keep.

Companionship with the Poor

And yet, moral heroics are not what are called for. Indeed, the transition required of the non-poor in entering into solidarity with the poor is not primarily a moral imperative at all. The difficulty for the non-poor in growing in faith is at least as much one of vision as it is one of will. And vision is a matter of vantage point. Our sensibilities as well as our blind spots, the expectations others have of us and that we have of ourselves, the challenges we come to recognize as opportunities for growth, the people to whom we feel accountable, the agenda of our lives—all are shaped according to where we stand on the social pyramid. From the vantage point of power we get a certain perspective on reality. It is the inheritance of all who have been born, educated, and successfully socialized into the system.

As long as we move habitually within the circles of privilege we are insulated from the experience of the poor. Closed to that experience, there is no reason to anticipate that we should be touched by the expectations of the poor, instructed by their perceptions, caught up in their agenda or drawn in any sustained fashion into the companionship of those laboring to build the just society. And yet that is what maturing in faith is all about. A moral commitment may attract us to this endeavor and even convince us that we are part of it, but, confined to our own social class, we are prisoners of our own perception of things. And, as long as we are prisoners of our own perceptions, whatever we are about will not be the building of the just society.

Our perception of things is a social rather than a purely individual construction. It grows out of the social interaction that has shaped our lives. Consequently, we can break out of it only in the course of a different kind of social interaction. Good will is no substitute for this interaction: we can come to a new vision only in a new companionship. We grow in understanding only as we are touched by the experience of those whose experience has never before touched us. We grow in faith only as we enter a communion we have never shared before. We shed the prejudices of power only as we are instructed by the poor. This is not to romanticize the poor but to recognize that unless the new vision includes the vision of those who have been left out, unless the new faith includes their faith and celebrates the community in which they participate, then it is really no new vision, faith, or community but simply a variation of the old, a continued celebration of the present community of the favored.[7]

In Walter Broderick's biography of Camilo Torres, martyred in the struggle for justice in Colombia in 1966, we get a telling description of this shift—from one companionship to another—which marks a maturing faith:

What distinguished Camilo from those around him was his zeal for drawing closer to the workers, not his intellectual talents.... Marxist pundits poked friendly gibes at him, and government technocrats smiled indulgently, and Catholic prelates clicked their tongues, and bad-tempered politicians snorted and all of them, one by one, began to close their doors on him. As they did so, other doors, opened, doors improvised out of cardboard tacked on a frame, or packing-case panels or sheets of rusty corrugated iron.[8]

Growing in faith means growing out of our privileged isolation from the experience of most of the world's people, the world's poor. The Gospel gives us no reason to expect it would be otherwise. In the incarnation tradition, God is with the people, divine life stirring among the masses. The poor are the medium of God's graciousness. Any who would be graced will stand with them.

And indeed, if we grow we will have been graced. Growth, at least growth in faith, is not the reward of moral exertion. As many foreign and urban missionaries could attest, sharing the experience of the poor is not something that can simply be chosen. Circumstances of birth and socialization impose real restrictions on the ability of the affluent to choose solidarity with the poor. To ignore those limits is to leave ourselves open to romanticism and self-delusion. Rather than affecting to share the experience of the oppressed as if it were a matter within our control, we are invited by the Gospel to surrender our control. Because it is our ability to control our lives that most distinguishes us from the poor, companionship with them is conditional on our relinquishing that control.

To accept responsibility not only for our ideas but for our choices, to gather with those who would build the just society, to stay at the meeting until some action is decided on, to accept a task and see it through to the end, is to risk losing control of our time, our priorities, our freedom to plan our lives. It is to risk discovering that our resources and energies are not our own, that these things belong to the people. There will always be reasons enough for us to hold back, to husband our resources, to remain captains of our own ship. There will be mortgage payments and family responsibilities to be met. This will not be the right time to act, nor this the right cause, nor these the right people. Serious reservations, all of them, but then faith matures only in the teeth of serious reservations.

To surrender our control, and the security and connections that guarantee it, is to embark on a faithful journey. It is a journey that promises to bring us gradually near enough to the poor—geographically as well as spiritually—to know them, to enter into human interaction with them, to recognize their aspirations, to sense the depth of their discontent, the urgency of their needs, the nature of their hope. Only then can we make available to them what skills and resources we have, as they ask for them and for the purposes they intend. Companionship with the poor is not a rampart we are called to storm: it is a grace to which we are invited to open ourselves.

Building the community in which all the world's people can gather for their lives is the present, pressing responsibility of faith; and helping people assume that responsibility is the task of ministry. It is not a task for isolated initiative but for the pooled ideas, resources, experiences, criticism, imagination, and artistry of a faithful community. Those of us who contemplate the task from privileged enclaves will need to learn from those who have already ventured out, those who have found ways to put their persons and professions at the disposal of the poor. It is the task to which we are summoned by the universal church, and a measure of the vitality of the local church. It is a summons to mature in faith. As a call to faithfulness, it will not be felt as a burdensome moral imperative compelling us to quixotic or "heroic" responses, but as an invitation to enter into a richer, more sustaining community with those who struggle to be free and, in so doing, to discover for ourselves the truth that sets us free.

The Maturing of the Local Church

How the local church will respond to that invitation is not a question that arises in a vacuum. It arises in the context of the existing faith community—with its traditional membership, priorities, and expectations. Some may be ready for the unsettling process of development to a new stage of faith but many may not, as became evident to Catholics when Vatican II first challenged the relatively dependent faith of the preconciliar parish and religious order. A similar challenge faces the church today, the challenge of development. Where that challenge has been taken up—in the U.S. Catholic church, communities of women religious appear to have been the readiest to do it—it has not been without pain and some division. Where the challenge has been laid aside, as it seems to have been in the vast majority of parishes, the reason commonly cited is the need to maintain the harmony of the existing community and the integrity of its traditional membership. It is not a question of being insensitive to the need for change, but of being sensitive to "where the people are at," of not alienating people, not moving too quickly.

There are real issues at stake here. One is that, where people are not ready for change, they will rightly be alienated by change forced on them from outside. The growth of the community in faith has

nothing to do with coercion. It has much to do, however, with the openness of the community to change,
its willingness to redefine its membership, its readi-
ness for a wider companionship. In the case of faith
communities already embraced and favored by the
existing structures of global power, maturing in faith
will entail their dismantling the structures that keep
the others out. The worship of the God beyond the
gods of tribe, class, and nation will be discovered only
in the company of those who are open to a community
beyond tribe, class, and nation. To what extent is the
local church challenging its members to undertake
this task? What support does it give those who are
ready to enter this wider companionship? What hope
does it represent for those who still stand outside the
community of the favored? These are the tests of its
quality as a community of living faith.

What is to be said, then, of faith communities that
shrink from the challenge of development, of parishes
bound in solidarity against the outsider, of dioceses
addressing oppression with little but lyrical pro-
nouncement, of a church too close to the mighty to
want companionship with the weak? Because faith is
essentially a living process, when it fails to develop it
begins to die. It will scarcely matter that the harmony
of the parish has been maintained if the sword that
might have divided it is the Gospel. It will be a trifling
achievement for faith if, while we enjoy new freedom
in the post-conciliar church, the global structures of
bondage remain untouched. Our claims to have found
new "Spirit-filled" communities will be idle if we have
not found community with the oppressed. For they
are the bearers of the Spirit. Where the Spirit of God is
a life-giving Spirit, it blows no longer in societies

where the life-chances of some are consolidated against the participation of others. The life-giving Spirit blows only where the oppressed are battling to gain entry or being welcomed into a society in which the lives of all are cherished.

Notes

Chapter 1: The Challenge to Faith

1. Andrew M. Greeley, *The American Catholic: A Social Portrait* (New York: Basic Books, 1977).

2. Talcott Parsons, "Christianity," *International Encyclopedia of the Social Sciences*, 2:426–29.

3. Paul Tillich, *Political Expectations* (New York: Harper and Row, 1971), p.73; see also George H. Williams, "Priest, Prophet and Proletariat," *Journal of Liberal Religion* (Winter 1940).

4. Paul Heinisch, *Theology of the Old Testament* (Collegeville, Minn.: Liturgical Press, 1955), pp. 18–24.

5. Louis F. Hartman, "Prophet," *Encyclopedic Dictionary of the Bible* (New York: McGraw-Hill, 1963), p. 1935.

6. Plato, *Gorgias, Republic, Laws;* Aristotle, *Nicomachean Ethics.*

7. See the literature on "exchange theory," especially George Homans, "Social Behavior as Exchange," *American Journal of Sociology* 62 (1958).

8. See Robert Nozick, *Anarchy, State and Utopia* (New York: Basic Books, 1975).

9. See Sigmund Freud, *Civilization and its Discontents* (New York: W. W. Norton, 1962).

10. See Edward O. Wilson, *Sociobiology: The New Synthesis* (Cambridge, Mass.: Harvard University Press, 1975).

11. For the official Catholic response to contemporary social injustices, see Joseph Gremillion, ed., *The Gospel of Peace and Justice: Catholic Social Teaching since Pope John* (Maryknoll, N.Y.: Orbis Books, 1976).

12. The case is made by Andrew Greeley in *The American Catholic.*

13. Gordon Allport, *The Nature of Prejudice* (New York: Doubleday, 1958).

14. See Gerhard Lenski, *The Religious Factor* (Garden City, N.Y.: Anchor Books, 1963); Charles Y. Glock and Rodney Stark, *Christian Beliefs and Anti-Semitism* (New York: Harper Torchbooks, 1966); Charles Y. Glock et al., *To Comfort and to Challenge* (Berkeley: University of California Press, 1967).

15. Thomas Pettigrew and Ernest Campbell, *Christians in Racial Crisis* (Washington, D.C.: Public Affairs Press, 1957).

16. Dean Kelley, *Why the Conservative Churches Are Growing* (New York: Harper and Row, 1972). The Gallup Poll shows the decline in Catholic attendance well in evidence before the end of the fifties—about the time when the official Catholic church began newly addressing itself to human and civil rights issues. See *Religion in America 1975: Gallup Opinion Index*, Report No. 114: "Church Attendance in an Average Week."

17. While this seems to me a fair characterization of the charismatic movement generally, one should not overlook the concern among a few charismatics and evangelicals for institutionalized evil and social transformation. See, for example, Ralph Martin, *Hungry for God* (New York: Doubleday, 1974); Jim Wallis, *Agenda for Biblical People* (New York: Harper and Row, 1976); and *Sojourners*, the magazine of the People's Christian Coalition in Washington, D.C.

18. See, for example, Garrett Hardin, "Lifeboat Ethics: The Case Against Helping the Poor," *Psychology Today*, September 1974.

19. Synod of Bishops, "Justice in the World," in Gremillion, ed., *The Gospel of Peace and Justice*. In a celebrated passage, the bishops state: "Action on behalf of justice and participation in the transformation of the world fully appear to us as a constitutive dimension of the preaching of the Gospel, or, in other words, of the church's mission for the redemption of the human race and its liberation from every oppressive situation" (Introduction, no. 6).

Chapter 2: How Faith Develops

1. See Robert N. Bellah, *Beyond Belief* (New York: Harper and Row, 1970), pp. 222–23.

2. Paul Tillich, "Trends in Religious Thought that Affect Social Outlook," *Religion and World Order*, ed. F. E. Johnson (New York: Harper, 1944), p. 17.

3. Paul Tillich, *Theology of Culture*, ed. Robert C. Kimball (London: Oxford University Press, 1959), p. 40.

4. No doubt the name best associated with this kind of analysis—called structural analysis—is that of Swiss psychologist Jean Piaget.

5. Best known in this area is the work of Harvard educationist Lawrence Kohlberg.

6. Pioneering research in this area is being done by theologian James W. Fowler of Emory University. Whether the structures of faith as described by Fowler finally prove to be universal is a matter that will require much more extensive empirical research than has yet been undertaken. It seems likely that at least the present *description* of the six stages of faith outlined by Fowler will need modification as more interviews are conducted among people of eastern faith traditions.

7. See Jean Piaget, *Six Psychological Studies* (New York: Vintage Books, 1968), especially David Elkind's introduction. Also Herbert Ginsburg and Sylvia Opper, *Piaget's Theory of Intellectual*

Development (Englewood Cliffs, N.J.: Prentice Hall, 1969), pp. 18–19.

8. See Lawrence Kohlberg, "Stage and Sequence," *Handbook of Socialization Theory and Research*, ed. David A. Goslin (Chicago: Rand McNally, 1969), p. 349; Jean Piaget, "The General Problems of the Psychobiological Development of the Child," *Discussions on Child Development*, ed. J. M. Tanner and B. Inhelder (New York: International Universities Press, 1960), 4:3–27.

9. Jean Piaget, *The Moral Judgment of the Child* (New York: Free Press, 1965).

10. Speaking of faith development from the aspect of changes in "role-taking ability and extensiveness of identification," Fowler explains: "This variable focuses on the person's way of constructing the inner motivations, intentions and feelings of other persons. It begins with initial ego-centrism. Then, developmentally it leads through mutual role-taking and eventually to the ability to take the role of other groups and of their worldviews. This development is correlated with a gradual expansion in the inclusion of other persons and groups in one's reference community, and moves toward a meaningful sense of membership in a universal commonwealth of being" (James W. Fowler, "Stages in Faith: The Structural Developmental Approach," *Values and Moral Development*, ed. Thomas C. Hennessy, New York: Paulist Press, 1976, p. 180). For other recent statements of his theory, see Fowler, "Faith Development Theory and the Aims of Religious Socialization," *Emerging Issues in Religious Education*, ed. Gloria Durka and Joanmarie Smith (New York: Paulist Press, 1976); and Fowler, "Mapping Faith's Structures: A Developmental Overview," *Life-Maps: The Human Journey of Faith*, ed. Sam Keen and Jerome Berryman (Needham, Mass.: Humanitas Press, 1976).

The same process is clearly apparent in Kohlberg's description of the development of moral judgment. The first four stages of the Kohlberg model represent the individual's more and more adequate recognition of the demands of the wider society. Nor does the process stop there: the "principled" thinking of the final two stages implies a moving beyond even social norms to universal principles of justice, principles to which both society and the self owe allegiance. The increased role-taking ability involves the capacity to take, first, the perspective of other individuals, then the perspective of society and, finally, a universal humanistic perspective. See Lawrence Kohlberg, "Stage and Sequence," pp. 347–480; "From Is to Ought," *Cognitive Development and Epistemology*, ed. T. Mischel (New York: Academic Press, 1971).

11. This grossly describes the movement of Fowler's six stages of development; it is similar to Kohlberg's model and has its roots in Piaget.

12. In this regard, Fowler comments: "Above all we want to avoid the nefarious misuse of the stage theory that would make of it a value scale to determine the relative worth of persons and groups. Each stage may be *the* most appropriate stage for a particular person or group. Each stage describes a pattern of valuing, think-

ing, feeling and committing that is potentially worthy, serene and grace-ful" (Fowler, "Stages in Faith," p. 191).

13. Fowler has himself presented the developmental model as a yardstick for religious educators, a standard against which the educational goals of a particular faith tradition might be evaluated (Fowler, "Faith Development Theory and the Aims of Religious Socialization").

14. Paulo Freire, *Pedagogy of the Oppressed* (New York: Herder and Herder, 1970).

Chapter 3: How Faith Gets Sidetracked

1. The liberal faith in the power of developing consciousness to bring about the just society leads us to the heart of a great historical debate, one which sprang to life in nineteenth-century Europe and in which we still inevitably take sides. It involves two philosophers whom we may not readily identify with the concerns of the local parish but whose theories are of critical importance to our understanding of the Christian life. They are Georg Wilhelm Friedrich Hegel, who lived in Germany from 1770 to 1831, and Karl Marx, who was just thirteen at the time of Hegel's death and who lived—for much of the time in England—until 1883. As in the model of development which we have been considering, Hegel's philosophy focuses on the profound changes of which the human mind is capable, and it is in this adaptability of the mind that he invests his hope for human society. His image of development, too, is one of the mind progressively shedding its limitations, in a movement towards more universal thinking, with all the implications that this carries for social justice. For Hegel, the vision of the whole which is grasped in thinking cries out for realization in history. This is how freedom and justice are won. The social and political institutions that grow out of our limited, prejudiced visions need to be dismantled in favor of those institutions that more nearly reflect the universal vision. Marx wrote of Hegel in 1844 that "he stands the world on its head and therefore can dissolve all barriers in his head, while of course they continue to endure for the actual human being." He meant by this that Hegel based historical change on changes in consciousness. But Marx saw that the real barriers that divide human beings from one another are not just barriers existing inside people's heads; they are barriers built into the social relations that frame our lives, and they are barriers quite capable of surviving through many changes in consciousness. Hegel's argument can be found in compendious form in his lectures on the philosophy of history, published as *Reason in History* (Indianapolis: Bobbs Merrill, 1953). Marx's argument can be found in the excerpt from his essay on "The German Ideology," in Karl Marx and Friedrich Engels, *Basic Writings on Politics and Philosophy*, ed. Lewis S. Feuer (New York: Anchor Books, 1959).

2. In this regard, it should be noted that the structures with which developmentalists are typically concerned are *psychic*

structures, structures of the mind—more specifically, cognitive structures. Growth is a matter of knowing better. In Kohlberg's metaphor, for example, the growing individual is essentially a philosopher (Lawrence Kohlberg and Rochelle Mayer, "Development as the Aim of Education," *Harvard Educational Review* 42 [November 1972]:456). While Fowler stresses the relational character of faith, it is usually assumed that new patterns of social relatedness can be expected to "flow from" new patterns of thinking and valuing ("Stages in Faith," pp. 175, 177). Successive stages of faith—like Kohlberg's successive stages of moral judgment—name successive, more differentiated interpretations of the world, each new interpretation better able to integrate new data and perspectives. But it is a model of more and more adequate *interpretations* rather than of more and more adequate structures of social relatedness. As in the case of Kohlberg's model, its criteria of adequacy are philosophical rather than social.

3. Figures are from the 1977 World Population Data Sheet, published by the Population Reference Bureau, Inc., 1337 Connecticut Ave., N.W., Washington, D.C. 20036.

4. It is quite wrong to think of consciousness as enjoying an independent life of its own, Marx argues, because it is always the consciousness of people situated at a certain point in the structure of society. Whether we are speaking of faith, morality, or philosophy, these ideas do not develop under their own steam. What we have is a certain pattern of human relationships, a certain system for getting the jobs done that need to be done to maintain society, and the ideas that gain currency at any time reflect that pattern of relationships. It is not the system that flows from the ideas, but rather the ideas that flow from the system. "Life is not determined by consciousness, but consciousness by life" (Marx and Engels, *Basic Writings*, p. 247).

5. Marx criticized religion as a tool used by the ruling classes to pacify the masses. His argument, including his description of religion as "the opium of the people," is found in summary form in the excerpt from "Toward the Critique of Hegel's Philosophy of Right," in Marx and Engels, *Basic Writings*, pp. 262–66. In a similar vein, the celebrated German sociologist Max Weber argues that, for the poor, religion functions to divert their hopes away from this world and focus them on another world, a distant heaven, as the only place where they might be realized. His argument may be found in his *The Sociology of Religion* (Boston: Beacon Press, 1964), a work published first in 1922, in which he describes the uses of religion in the class society or, as he puts it, "certain characteristic contrasts in what religion must provide for the various social strata" (see especially pp. 97–103, 106–7, 117).

6. Weber argues that, while religion displaces the hopes of the poor to another world and stokes up the enthusiasm of working people for the wearying routines required to keep the system going, it functions for the educated as a way to resolve their problems of meaning. And a central problem that faith will have to help with,

according to Weber, is that of how to feel justified as an advantaged person in a world where so many are disadvantaged (*The Sociology of Religion*). As pastors counsel the poor to be patient and hope for heaven because we cannot see any practical way out of their problems right now, as preachers reassure their working-class families on Sunday morning that God blesses their persevering labor and good citizenship, or as the suburban study-group wrestles with Tillich's *Courage to Be*, Weber's argument is illustrated. The religion that he describes is religion tailored to the needs of the class society.

7. It may well be argued that there are evils that precede society's woes and that would remain even if society's woes were resolved. To say that faith must address itself to the human ills consequent upon the social conditions of life is not to say that they are the only human ills with which faith must reckon. Concern for social evil can be expected to lead to an awareness of the evil not reducible to societal choices—the existentialist evils of finitude and unrealizable aspirations. This kind of concern will evidence a mature faith, however, only if it takes up and embraces the quest for social justice, even while recognizing the limits of that quest. The concern for evil that would so explain social ills—for example, as a necessary result of the "nature of human finitude"—that the struggle for social justice would be undercut or bypassed should be assessed as a failure of faith. The distinguishing mark of a faith oriented to justice is not a sense of tragedy before the evils that transcend our choices (though that may be present), but a thirst for justice before the ills that reflect our choices.

Chapter 4: Faith and Community

1. On this point, sociologists Peter Berger and Thomas Luckmann write: "To have a conversion experience is nothing much. The real thing is to be able to keep on taking it seriously; to retain a sense of its plausibility. *This* is where the religious community comes in. It provides the indispensable plausibility structure for the new reality. In other words, Saul may have become Paul in the aloneness of religious ecstasy, but he could *remain* Paul only in the context of the Christian community that recognized him as such and confirmed the 'new being' in which he now located his identity" (*The Social Construction of Reality*, New York: Anchor Books, 1967, p. 158).

2. Life in any social group, British anthropologist Mary Douglas has written, is made intelligible and bearable only by reference to the group's cosmology or worldview. Our cosmology is made up of the categories that enable us to make sense of our place in the world—and other people's places—and to endure the suffering that comes our way. It is not a hard shell that the tortoise has to carry forever, she explains, but it is quite flexible. In the course of the normal stresses and strains experienced by any group, some ad-

justments will have to be made and some spare parts fitted. But, so closely tied is the cosmology to a particular social group, that any fundamental reorganization of the social group will require a reorganization of the cosmology. In this case, "a major overhaul is necessary to bring the obsolete set of views into focus with new times and new company. This is conversion" (*Natural Symbols*, New York: Vintage Books, 1973, p. 179).

3. The findings that follow are those of French sociologist Emile Durkheim who, at the turn of the century, produced a landmark study of the nature of religion in primitive societies. See Emile Durkheim, *The Elementary Forms of the Religious Life* (New York: Free Press, 1965; originally published in 1902).

4. See, for example, C. Wright Mills, *The Sociological Imagination* (New York: Oxford University Press, 1967); George H. Mead, *Mind, Self and Society* (Chicago: University of Chicago Press, 1962); Basil Bernstein, "Social Class and Psychotherapy," *British Journal of Sociology* 15 (1964): 54–64; Thomas Luckmann, *The Invisible Religion* (London: Macmillan, 1970); Peter L. Berger and Thomas Luckmann, *The Social Construction of Reality* (New York: Anchor Books, 1967).

5. Robert N. Bellah, *The Broken Covenant* (New York: Crossroads, 1975), p. 88.

6. Ibid., p. 55.

Chapter 5: Faith and Authenticity

1. Basil Bernstein, *Theoretical Studies Towards a Sociology of Language* (London: Routledge and Kegan Paul, 1971).

2. R. D. Laing, *The Politics of the Family* (New York: Vintage Books, 1972), p. 79.

3. For the importance to the modern industrial state of the internalizing by workers of the myth of hierarchy, see Max Horkheimer, *Critical Theory* (New York: Continuum, 1972); Richard J. Barnet and Ronald E. Müller, *Global Reach* (New York: Touchstone, 1974); and Richard Sennett and Jonathan Cobb, *The Hidden Injuries of Class* (New York: Knopf, 1972).

4. Laing, *Politics of the Family*, p. 82.

5. Harvey Cox describes the effect on the believer of this new dawning: "The shock of discovery may make him an agnostic. On the other hand, he may re-appropriate components of his religious heritage in an even more personal and conscious way. He may be totally taken in by the religions of the media, but he can never again be uncritically and unreflectively 'religious' in the traditional sense. He cannot go back to the tribe. The secular city man may still remember the old stories and symbols, but he recognizes them as such. This makes his religion, whatever it is, very different from the faith of the villager" (*The Seduction of the Spirit*, New York: Simon and Schuster, 1973, pp. 59–60).

Juan Luis Segundo, a Uruguayan theologian and one of the architects of Latin America's "liberation theology," points to this quality of authenticity in speaking of the need for believers to have wrestled with the questions raised by human experience if their faith is to be mature. The faith which has never had to face up to the hard questions is just a protective blanket of unexamined myth. Segundo writes: "We Christians believe that any pathway toward authenticity in our being and life is a preparation for the gospel. . . . We can act to avoid the risk of thinking. . . . To live life deeply, to take our existence in our own hands, to fashion ourselves consciously and fully—this is the difficult road to take, the 'narrow gate' that leads us to a simple but unendingly profound question: Who are we? . . . Without this growth in authenticity . . . the proclamation of the faith is in danger of being turned into an ideology or a myth" (*The Community Called Church*, Maryknoll, N.Y.: Orbis Books, 1973, pp. 67–68).

6. A recent pitch by *Playboy* for business advertising suggests how vacuous the apparently radical aspirations of the late sixties could turn out to be. "Good news for American business," it trumpeted. "Those young men who wouldn't sell out in 1967 are buying in in 1977." It went on:

"You know those young men we're talking about. They're the ones who were marching up and down their campuses protesting a war, forcing a President out of office, putting barber shops all over America out of business for lack of business.

"They were remarkable then, intense and totally committed even as teenagers. A generation that had an earlier awareness of what was going on around them than any generation in our history.

"And what's even more remarkable about them is that today, ten years later, they haven't lost one iota of that intensity.

"They've just totally redirected it.

"They've traded the SDS for IBM. . . . They've joined the establishment. In fact, they're on their way to leading it" (*New York Times*, February 11, 1977).

7. Rollo May, *Paulus* (New York: Harper and Row, 1973), p. 89.

8. *The Autobiography of Malcolm X* (New York: Grove Press, 1965).

9. Cox, *Seduction of the Spirit*, pp. 115, 118–19.

10. Paulo Freire, *Pedagogy of the Oppressed* (New York: Herder and Herder, 1970), pp. 32–33, 60.

11. Ronald J. Wilkins, *Understanding Christian Morality*, a text in the *To Live Is Christ* series (Dubuque: William C. Brown, 1972), p. 178.

12. Robert N. Bellah, "The Historical Background of Unbelief," *The Culture of Unbelief*, ed. Rocco Caporale and Antonio Grumelli (Berkeley: University of California Press, 1971), p. 47.

13. N. J. Demerath, III, *A Tottering Transcendence* (Indianapolis: Bobbs-Merrill, 1974), p. 35; Thomas Luckmann, *The Invisible Religion* (London: Macmillan, 1970), pp. 97, 110, 116; Peter L. Berger, *The Sacred Canopy* (Garden City, N.Y.: Anchor Books, 1969), pp. 133–34.

Chapter 6: Faith and Justice

1. See editorial, "Calling Western Philly!" *National Catholic Reporter*, January 7, 1977, p. 8; editorial, "Happiness is our Parish," *NCR*, January 21, 1977, p. 13; "Repartee," *NCR*, January 28, 1977, pp. 10–11.

2. In this regard, theologian Letty M. Russell writes: "Oppressed groups are not in a position to dialogue with the oppressor groups because the process of dialogue only functions where there is a situation of equality and trust. 'If you want to talk with me, take your foot off my neck!' First, the oppressed groups must develop their own power base of mutual support, new identity, and new possibility for collective action. They must search together for their own liberation according to their own agenda, because liberation is not a commodity to be given away. It is a process of new awareness and action that grows out of new personal and collective consciousness" *(Human Liberation in a Feminist Perspective*, Philadelphia: Westminster Press, 1974, p. 68).

3. James H. Cone, *A Black Theology of Liberation* (Philadelphia: Lippincott, 1970), p. 26.

4. See, for example, Gustavo Gutiérrez, *A Theology of Liberation* (Maryknoll, N.Y.: Orbis Books, 1973), p. 137.

5. See Richard J. Neuhaus, "Liberation Theology and the Captivities of Jesus," *Worldview*, June 1973, pp. 41–48.

6. On the relationship between universal love and class struggle, Gutiérrez writes: "To deny the fact of class struggle is really to put oneself on the side of the dominant sectors. Neutrality is impossible. It is not a question of admitting or denying a fact which confronts us; rather it is a question of which side we are on. . . . The Gospel announces the love of God for all people and calls us to love as he loves. But to accept class struggle means to decide for some and against others. To live both realities without juxtaposition is a great challenge for the Christian committed to the totality of the process of liberation. . . . Universal love is that which in solidarity with the oppressed seeks also to liberate the oppressors from their own power, from their ambition, and from their selfishness. . . . This is the challenge, as new as the Gospel: to love our enemies. . . . It is not a question of having no enemies, but rather of not excluding them from our love. But love does not mean that the oppressors are no longer enemies, nor does it eliminate the radicalness of the combat against them. . . . To participate in class struggle not only is not opposed to universal love; this commitment is today the necessary and inescapable means of making this love concrete. . . . The communion of paschal joy passes through confrontation and the cross" *(Theology of Liberation*, pp. 274–76).

7. Ibid., p. 49.

8. "There is no universalism," Cone contends, "that is not particular. Indeed the insistence by white theologians upon the universal note of the Gospel arises out of their own particular political

and social interests. As long as they can be sure that the Gospel is *for everybody*—ignoring that God liberated a *particular* people from Egypt, came in a particular man called Jesus and for the particular purpose of liberating the oppressed—they can continue to talk in theological abstractions, failing to recognize that such talk is not the Gospel unless it is related to the concrete freedom of the little ones" (James H. Cone, "Who is Jesus Christ for Us Today?" *Christianity and Crisis*, April 14, 1975, pp. 84–85).

9. See Henri J. M. Nouwen, "Reflections on Political Ministry," *Network Quarterly* 4 (Fall 1976), p. A1; and Wayne H. Cowan and Vivian Lindermayer, "An Anniversary Statement," *Christianity and Crisis* 36 (November 15, 1976), p. 259.

Chapter 7: Faith and Affluence

1. Wilkins, *Understanding Morality*, p. 179. The full description reads: "Mr. McLemore, president of the bank, is the very picture of a successful banker. He is driven to work in a chauffeured foreign car, smokes expensive cigars, and wears carefully tailored suits. He gets to work before his employees and leaves only when everyone else is gone. He is kind and generous to everyone, especially to those who work for him. He knows everyone by name, knows their strengths and weaknesses, their problems and their hopes. He sees to it that their working conditions are pleasant and hires extra help so that everyone gets a surprise long weekend every so often. Three nights a week he devotes to what he calls 'community challenges.' He heads the 'Community Chest Drive' for the underprivileged, is a member of the school board, and chairman of the park district planning committee. Twice each summer he opens his home, grounds, and swimming pool to the handicapped children in his suburban area. His company Christmas party is a gift-giving event for the poorest families of the ghetto which fringes on the prosperous business district in which his bank is located. He doesn't seek publicity for his many activities, and never allows his name to appear with his position as president of the bank in any publicity associated with his community work. He doesn't protest when vulgar, uninformed pickets march in front of his bank carrying obscene and insulting placards shouting, 'Mr. McLemore, dirty capitalist pig! Exploiter of the poor! Slave master of the worker class!' 'Let them have their kicks,' he says to his wife and friends. 'I'd rather do than protest.' Mr. McLemore's four children think he's pretty cool. His only house rule is, 'Be polite to each other. Civility and kindness are the mark of character. Anybody can scream and yell and throw a temper tantrum. These things we do not do here or at work.' "

2. Gérard Lutte, "How to Preach the Gospel to the Rich," *World Parish* 16 (March 1976).

3. Marie Augusta Neal, S.N.D.deN., *A Socio-Theology of Letting-Go: The Role of a First World Church Facing Third World Peoples* (New York: Paulist, 1977).

4. Gutiérrez, *Theology of Liberation*, p. 300.

5. Lutte suggests the full import for faith of the Gospel categories of rich and poor: "The rich are not only those who possess an abundance of material goods. The category includes all those who find themselves above another human being and who make use of their power to dominate and manipulate other human beings—whether that power is based on force, authority, social position, knowledge, prestige, or what have you. The poor, on the other hand, are those who live in friendship with others, sharing what they have with those in need and placing their knowledge and talent at the service of others. Friendship presupposes equality. The boss, the man in power, the member of some hierarchy cannot be a friend of people who are under him."

Regarding the political distinction between capitalist and proletariat, Lutte points out that it does not coincide exactly with the Gospel distinction between rich and poor: "To be sure, the capitalist is one of the rich in the gospel sense because he uses people as instruments to increase his own power and wealth. But there are many other forms of oppression and violence besides those of capitalism and imperialism: the oppression of male over female, of adult over child, of the educated over the uneducated, of the strong over the weak. Members of the proletariat may behave like medieval lords or bosses at home, or betray their class solidarity as scabs, or try to get away from their class and acquire the unjust privileges of the ruling class. Members of the proletariat are not necessarily poor people in the gospel sense; capitalists never are" ("How to Preach the Gospel to the Rich").

6. Drawing a veil in this way over the nature of the class society, Georg Lukács points out, is essential to maintaining that kind of society: "For the insoluble internal contradictions of the system become revealed with increasing starkness and so confront its supporters with a choice. Either they must consciously ignore insights which become increasingly urgent or else they must suppress their own moral instincts in order to be able to support with a good conscience an economic system that serves only their own interests" (*History and Class Consciousness*, Cambridge, Mass.: Massachusetts Institute of Technology, 1971, p. 66).

Similarly, Neal points to the choice pressed upon the theologian in a divided world: "The theologian has to choose a standpoint from which to begin viewing. It makes all the difference in the world where one stands—whether one stands, that is, beside the rich or beside the poor. In a divided world, one would have to be God, or at least standing beside God, to stand simultaneously with both groups. The perspectives are too different to allow one to bilocate" ("Civil Religion, Theology and Politics in America," in *America in Theological Perspective*, ed. Thomas M. McFadden, New York: Seabury, 1976, p. 108).

7. For this reason it is imperative, as Freire insists, that the naming of reality be done by the oppressed coming to critical consciousness. See *Pedagogy of the Oppressed*, p. 76.

8. Walter J. Broderick, *Camilo Torres: A Biography of the Priest-Guerrillero* (Garden City N.Y.: Doubleday, 1975), p. 186.

Bibliography

Allport, Gordon. *The Nature of Prejudice*. New York: Doubleday, 1958.

Assmann, Hugo. "Basic Aspects of Theological Reflection in Latin America: Critical Evaluation of the Theology of Liberation." Paper presented at the World Council of Churches Symposium, *Black Theology and Latin American Theology of Liberation*, May 1–4, 1973, and published in *Risk*, magazine of the World Council of Churches, 9 (1973):25–33.

Barnet, Richard J., and Ronald E. Müller. *Global Reach: The Power of the Multinational Corporations*. New York: Touchstone, 1974.

Baum, Gregory. *Religion and Alienation: A Theological Reading of Sociology*. New York: Paulist, 1976.

Bellah, Robert N. *Beyond Belief: Essays on Religion in a Post-Traditional World*. New York: Harper and Row, 1970.

———. "The Historical Background of Unbelief." In *The Culture of Unbelief: Studies and Proceedings from the First International Symposium on Belief*, Rome, March 22–27, 1969. Ed. Rocco Caporale and Antonio Grumelli. Berkeley: University of California Press, 1971, pp. 39–52.

———. *The Broken Covenant: American Civil Religion in Time of Trial*. New York: Seabury (Crossroad), 1975.

Berger, Peter L. *The Sacred Canopy: Elements of a Sociological Theory of Religion*. Garden City, N.Y.: Anchor Books, 1969.

———, and Thomas Luckmann. *The Social Construction of Reality: A Treatise in the Sociology of Knowledge*. Garden City, N.Y.: Anchor Books, 1967.

Bernstein, Basil. "Social Class and Psychotherapy." *British Journal of Sociology* 15 (1964): 54–64.

———. *Theoretical Studies Towards a Sociology of Language*. London: Routledge and Kegan Paul, 1971.

Cone, James H. *A Black Theology of Liberation*. Philadelphia: Lippincott, 1970.

Cox, Harvey. *The Seduction of the Spirit: The Use and Mis-*

use of People's Religion. New York: Simon and Schuster, 1973.

―――. "The Boston Affirmations." *Christianity and Crisis* 36 (February 16, 1976).

Demerath, N. J., III. *A Tottering Transcendence: Civil vs. Cultic Aspects of the Sacred.* Indianapolis: Bobbs-Merrill, 1974.

Douglas, Mary. *Natural Symbols: Explorations in Cosmology.* New York: Vintage Books, 1973.

Durka, Gloria, and Joanmarie Smith, eds. *Emerging Issues in Religious Education.* New York: Paulist, 1976.

Durkheim, Emile. *Suicide.* Glencoe, Ill.: Free Press, 1951.

―――. *The Elementary Forms of the Religious Life.* Trans. Joseph W. Swain. New York: Free Press, 1965.

―――. *Selected Writings.* Ed., trans., and intro. by Anthony Giddens. Cambridge: Cambridge University Press, 1972.

Einaudi, Luigi, et al. "Latin American Institutional Development: The Changing Catholic Church." Memorandum prepared for the Office of External Research, U.S. Department of State, RM-6136-DOS. The Rand Corporation, October 1969.

Fowler, James W. "Faith, Liberation and Human Development." *The Foundation,* quarterly published by Gammon Theological Seminary, Atlanta, 79 (Spring 1974).

―――. *To See the Kingdom: The Theological Vision of H. Richard Niebuhr.* Nashville: Abingdon, 1974.

―――. "Faith Development Theory and the Aims of Religious Socialization." *Emerging Issues in Religious Education.* Ed. Gloria Durka and Joanmarie Smith. New York: Paulist, 1976.

―――. "Mapping Faith's Structures: A Developmental Overview." *Life-Maps: The Human Journey of Faith.* Ed. Sam Keen and Jerome Berryman. Needham, Mass.: Humanitas Press, 1976.

―――. "Stages in Faith: The Structural-Developmental Approach." *Values and Moral Development.* Ed. Thomas C. Hennessy. New York: Paulist, 1976.

Freire, Paulo. *Pedagogy of the Oppressed.* Trans. Myra Bergman Ramos. New York: Herder and Herder, 1970.

Freud, Sigmund. *Civilization and Its Discontents.* New York: W. W. Norton, 1962.

Ginsburg, Herbert, and Sylvia Opper. *Piaget's Theory of Intellectual Development: An Introduction.* Englewood Cliffs, N.J.: Prentice-Hall, 1969.

Glock, Charles Y., et al. *To Comfort and to Challenge: A Dilemma of the Contemporary Church.* Berkeley: University of California Press, 1967.

————, and Rodney Stark. *Christian Beliefs and Anti-Semitism: A Scientific Study of the Way Christian Beliefs Shape American Attitudes towards the Jews* (New York: Harper and Row, 1969).

Gremillion, Joseph. *The Gospel of Peace and Justice: Catholic Social Teachings Since Pope John.* Maryknoll, N.Y.: Orbis Books, 1976.

Gutiérrez, Gustavo. *A Theology of Liberation: History, Politics and Salvation.* Trans. Sr. Caridad Inda and John Eagleson. Maryknoll, N.Y.: Orbis, 1973.

Harrington, Michael. *Socialism.* New York: Bantam, 1973.

Hartman, Louis F. "Prophet." *Encyclopedic Dictionary of the Bible.* New York: McGraw Hill, 1963, pp. 1930–38.

Heinisch, Paul. *Theology of the Old Testament.* Collegeville, Minn.: Liturgical Press, 1955.

Hennessy, Thomas C., ed. *Values and Moral Development.* New York: Paulist, 1976.

Homans, George. "Social Behavior as Exchange." *American Journal of Sociology* 62 (1958).

Horkheimer, Max. *Critical Theory: Selected Essays.* New York: Continuum, 1972.

Kegan, Robert. "Ego and Truth: Personality and the Piaget Paradigm." Unpublished doctoral dissertation, Harvard University, 1977.

Kelley, Dean. *Why the Conservative Churches are Growing.* New York: Harper and Row, 1972.

Keniston, Kenneth. *The Uncommitted: Alienated Youth in American Society.* New York: Dell, 1965.

Kohlberg, Lawrence. "Stage and Sequence: The Cognitive-Developmental Approach to Socialization." *Handbook of Socialization Theory and Research.* ed. David A. Goslin. Chicago: Rand McNally, 1969. pp. 347–480.

————. "From Is to Ought: How to Commit the Naturalistic Fallacy and Get Away with It in the Study of Moral Development." *Cognitive Development and Epistemology.* Ed. T. Mischel. New York: Academic Press, 1971.

————, and Rochelle Mayer. "Development as the Aim of Education." *Harvard Educational Review* 42 (November, 1972):448–96.

Laing, R. D. *The Politics of the Family.* New York: Vintage Books, 1972.

Lenski, Gerhard. *The Religious Factor: A Sociological Study of Religion's Impact on Politics, Economics and Family Life.* Garden City, N.Y.: Anchor Books, 1963.

Luckmann, Thomas. *The Invisible Religion: The Problem of Religion in Modern Society.* London: Macmillan, 1970.

Lukács, Georg. *History and Class Consciousness: Studies in Marxist Dialectics.* Cambridge: Massachusetts Institute of Technology, 1971.

Lutte, Gérard. "How to Preach the Gospel to the Rich." *World Parish* 16 (March 1976).

Mainelli, Vincent P., ed. *Social Justice! The Catholic Position.* Washington, D.C.: Consortium, 1975.

Mannheim, Karl. *Ideology and Utopia: An Introduction to the Sociology of Knowledge.* New York: Harcourt, Brace and World, 1936.

Marx, Karl, and Friedrich Engels. *Basic Writings on Politics and Philosophy.* Ed. Lewis S. Feuer. New York: Anchor Books. 1959.

May, Rollo. *Paulus: Reminiscences of a Friendship.* New York: Harper and Row, 1973.

Mead, George H. *Mind, Self and Society: From the Standpoint of a Social Behaviorist.* Ed. Charles W. Morris. Chicago: University of Chicago Press, 1962.

Míguez Bonino, José. *Doing Theology in a Revolutionary Situation.* Philadelphia: Fortress, 1975.

Mills, C. Wright. *The Sociological Imagination.* New York: Oxford University Press, 1967.

Neal, Marie Augusta, S.N.D. de N. "Socio-Anthropological Aspects of Religious Ministry." Paper presented at the Institute on Ministry and Orders, Notre Dame University, Indiana, June 1973.

———. "Civil Religion, Theology and Politics in America." *America in Theological Perspective.* Ed. Thomas M. McFadden. New York: Seabury, 1976, pp. 99–122.

———. *A Socio-Theology of Letting Go: The Role of a First World Church Facing Third World Peoples.* New York: Paulist Press, 1977.

Neuhaus, Richard J. "Liberation Theology and the Captivities of Jesus." *Worldview* 43 (1973): 41–48.

Nozick, Robert. *Anarchy, State and Utopia.* New York: Basic Books, 1975.

Parsons, Talcott. "Christianity." *International Encyclopedia of the Social Sciences*, 2:425–447.

Pettigrew, Thomas, and Ernest Campbell. *Christians in Racial Crisis*. Washington, D.C.: Public Affairs Press, 1957.

Piaget, Jean. "The General Problems of the Psychobiological Development of the Child." *Discussions on Child Development: Proceedings of the World Health Organization Study Group on the Psychobiological Development of the Child*. Ed. J. M. Tanner and B. Inhelder. New York: International Universities Press, 1960, 4:3–27.

———. *The Moral Judgment of the Child*. New York: Free Press, 1965.

———. *Six Psychological Studies*. New York: Vintage Books, 1968.

Ruether, Rosemary, et al. "Whatever Happened to Theology?" *Christianity and Crisis* 35 (May 12, 1975): 106–120.

Russell, Letty M. *Human Liberation in a Feminist Perspective: A Theology*. Philadelphia: Westminster, 1974.

Segundo, Juan Luis. *The Community Called Church*. Maryknoll, N.Y.: Orbis, 1973.

Sennett, Richard, and Jonathan Cobb. *The Hidden Injuries of Class*. New York: Knopf, 1972.

Sheehy, Gail. *Passages: Predictable Crises of Adult Life*. New York: E. P. Dutton, 1976.

Tillich, Paul. "Trends in Religious Thought that Affect Social Outlook," *Religion and World Order*. Ed. F. E. Johnson. New York: Harper, 1944.

———. *Dynamics of Faith*. New York: Harper Torchbooks, 1957.

———. *The Protestant Era*. Chicago: University of Chicago Press, 1957.

———. *Theology of Culture*. Ed. Robert C. Kimball. London: Oxford University Press, 1959.

———. *Political Expectations*. Ed. James Luther Adams. New York: Harper and Row, 1971.

Weber, Max. *The Sociology of Religion*. Trans. Ephraim Fischoff. Boston: Beacon, 1964.

Williams, George, H. "Priest, Prophet and Proletariat: A Study in the Theology of Paul Tillich." *Journal of Liberal Religion* (Winter 1940).

Wilson, Edward O. *Sociobiology: The New Synthesis*. Cambridge, Mass.: Harvard University Press, 1975.